Other books by James Prince

The Precious Princess of Wonderland
The True Face of The Antichrist
Always and Forever
Always And Forever + Ten Years Later
The Rough Road or The Golden Path?

WHY I HAVE TO DIE LIKE JESUS AND LOUIS RIEL?

JAMES PRINCE

www.trafford.com
North America & international
toll-free: 1 888 232 4444 (USA & Canada)
fax: 812 355 4082

DEDICATION

I dedicate this book to everyone who loves the true God with their whole heart and would like to do some work or something to help spreading the truth; meaning becoming a Jesus' disciple. If this is your case, please join me at: jamesprince@sasktel.net

See Webpages: jamesprinceauthor.com

Good luck

CHAPTER 1

The life of Louis Riel seen from a different angle.

I'd like to bring some light on Louis Riel's life, the light of the world. See Matthew 5, 14.

Louis Riel was also a salt container in the world and the world broke it down when he was executed. See Matthew 5, 13. 'You are the salt of the earth. But if the salt loses its saltiness, how can it be made salty again? It is no longer good for anything, except to be thrown out and trampled by men.'

Dozens of writers wrote about the life, the death and the career of Louis Riel, but they have mainly written about his politic activities and his rebellions. I will talk to you mainly about his relationship with God and that he had the same preoccupations than Jesus had in this world; meaning to free his people from the slavery of sin, the slavery of religion and to lead his people to God.

Louis Riel understood just like Jesus did that religions; mainly the one which has its head in Rome was a dreadful slavery and we definitely have to separate from it. This is the reason why the John A. MacDonald's government pressed by the Christian churches found a way to eliminate him from this earth despite the protestations against this execution and this from all over the world.

So, Louis Riel had to go through the same destiny than the one who inspired him; Jesus of Nazareth and this is why I expect the same conclusion for myself, because I do the same thing they did, meaning; opening the eyes of the blind.

Fortunately for the world and thanks to God a bit of salt and a gleam of light made their way up to me. So, in one way I'll be able to continue the work of the Jesus' disciples and this is what I'm doing with the help of my books and my songs.

We can't be sure of anything for what concerned the pass, but I have a strong impression a big part of the truth concerning the life and the career of Louis Riel was willingly hidden from the Canadian history and from the entire world and Louis Riel had nothing to do with this.

Louis Riel, the prophet of the new world as he called himself spent a lot of time with the priests, the bishops and the archbishops and I really believe this is what was fatal to him.

According to his story he studied in Montreal to become a priest. So according to the story still he had a chance to know about the Bible, the word of God, what is true in there and also what is false.

Knowing for myself that my grandfather some eighty some years ago was told by his priest not to let the children read the Bible, that they could go crazy if they do. Now we know that still according to the story Louis Riel was accused of mental illness and he spent a few years in St-Jean de Dieu in Montreal; an institution ran by the brothers and nuns, supervised by priests, bishops and archbishops. Riel also spent time in Beauport near Quebec City, another similar institution.

He was locked up on the pretension to protect him from the people who wanted to harm him when in fact he was held as a prisoner by the good nuns and friars. His good friend archbishop Taché did everything he could to keep Riel out of the circulation and after this, who would believe someone who was incarcerated for mental illness anyway?

He is crafty the enemy.

Since the beginning of his story the historians either they didn't understand or they didn't have the freedom to talk about it or yet they were afraid to do what I'm doing right now.

I think their life might have been at stake too knowing what happened to Louis Riel.

I understand I could also be accused of mental illness myself for doing this and also get death threats for daring challenging the history, the churches, the religions and the governments about all this.

Knowing the truth; especially the truth that contradicts the teaching of the Catholic Church or the Christian churches in general was and still is crazy for the ones who had to protect this institution and Louis Riel was in a position to cause a lot of damages to the credibility of Rome and to the clergy.

After having locked up a few priests and nuns who betrayed him and his people and taken control of his flock Louis Riel made the Saturday, the day of the Lord like the Law of God says and this was for me another important clue in my decision to write on this subject.

When we read in Exodus 20 from 8 to 11. 'Remember the Sabbath day, to keep it holy. Six days you shall labour and do all your work, but the seventh day is a Sabbath of the Lord your God, in it you shall not do any work, you or your son or your daughter, your male or female servant or your cattle or your sojourner who stays with you. For in six days the Lord made the heavens and the earth, the sea and all that is in them, and rested on the seventh day; therefore the Lord blessed the seventh day and made it holy.'

Knowing the week only holds seven days the seventh day has to be the last one and not the first. Anyone can understand the church doesn't teach the truth, the word of God when it teaches that the Sundays (first day of the week) you will keep serving the Lord. This might looks like nothing, but the last day is exactly contrary to the first.

We all know the devil likes to do things contrary to God and contrary to Jesus, whom we call the son of God. See what it's written in Matthew 5, 17-18 and I write; 'Do not think that I came to abolish the Law or the prophets; I did not come to abolish them, but to fulfill them. For truly I say to you, until heaven and earth pass away, not the smallest letter or stroke of a pen shall pass from the Law until all is accomplished.'

3

So the Law from which nothing has changed (word of God) since heaven and earth are still here, was changed for many people as far as the day of the Lord is concerned, but this was not done by the children of God, but rather by God's enemies.

I wrote a little song on the matter and it goes like this; they lied to me, they cheated me every Sunday morning. They lied to me; they cheated me, that's why I like to sing. The Lord told me the Sabbath day is Saturday, but the Sunday who is it for? Is there another lord? They lied to me, they cheated me.......

When we look a little about where the change came from, we can find very soon this was done by Paul. See Acts 20, 7. 'On the first day of the week, when we were gathered together to break bread, Paul began to talk to them.'

There is another reference in 1 Corinthians 16, 2. 'On the first day of every week each one of you is to put aside and save.'

One thing to notice here is the fact we don't talk about Saturday or Sunday, but about the first and the last day of the week. Jesus said that the one who annuls one of the least of these commandments from the Law and teach to do the same will be called the least in the kingdom of heaven. So I guess that according to Jesus I will be called great in the kingdom of heaven and Paul and his followers will be called at least, the least. You can read it in Matthew 5, 19. I'm sure too that Louis Riel is called great for he is.

No matter what the names of the week were in those days, the fact is the last day is contrary or opposite to the first.

So, according to what I just wrote, the Christian churches don't follow Jesus, the Christ, the word of God, but they follow Paul who opposed Jesus, which is antichrist.

The fact is also that Paul is opposed to God like the devil always is. Paul is opposed to God also about the circumcision, which is an everlasting covenant between God and men or his children, but of course the devil wanted to break this too. See Genesis 17, 13. 'A servant who is born in your house or who is bought with your money shall surely be circumcised; thus shall my covenant be in your flesh for an <u>everlasting</u> covenant.'

But the devil didn't like this and neither did Paul.

Take a look also in Genesis 9, 16. 'When the bow is in the cloud, then I will look upon it, to remember the everlasting covenant between God and every living creature of all flesh that is on the earth.'

Everlasting is like the bow that we can still see every so often after the rain and is existing since the big flood. Another everlasting covenant that will last forever and so is the circumcision. Go look in Paul's gospel to see how hard the devil try to destroy this everlasting covenant between God and men and you will find dozens of references like the one I will point out to you. You will find out this is quite a wish from a so called apostle. Open your Bible in Galatians 5, 12. 'I (Paul) wish that those (the circumcision group who was working hands and hands with the Jesus' apostles) who are troubling you would even mutilate themselves.'

I don't even think this is the worst from him. We all know the wish of God is the total opposite. Take a look at Genesis 1, 28. 'God blessed them, (people) and God said to them: Be fruitful and multiply and fill the earth and subdue it.'

But it takes a hypocrite to accuse the greatest of the apostles (Peter) wrongfully of hypocrisy. See acts 16, 3. 'Paul wanted this man (Timothy, the one he called his son) to go with him and he took him and he circumcised him because of the Jews who were in those parts, for they all knew that his father was a Greek.'

Poor Timothy, according to Paul himself in Galatians 5, 2, your are lost. 'Behold I, Paul say to you that if you receive circumcision, Christ will be of no benefit to you.'

This must be real sad to be condemned to hell by your own friend or your own father.

The truth is if you receive circumcision, the antichrist or the false christ will be of no benefit to you and this is rather a good thing.

I was blamed quite often for they say looking for ticks in the Bible, but Jesus said; 'Seek and you will find.'

If I found ticks in the Bible it wouldn't have been too bad, but finding lies and contradictions is rather distressful.

Well, you see I sought and I found and because I like to share with others my findings, here you are sharing my knowledge with me. I only hope this will fall in good soil and not in death ears or in a blind eye of a person who doesn't want to see and that it will produce lots of fruits for God, because He sent us many men and women so you can see.

There is another message in the Bible that comes to confirm the word of Jesus in Matthew 5, 17-18 and this one is from God Himself. You can read it in Jeremiah 31, 36. 'Only if these decrees vanish from my sight declares the Lord will the descendants of Israel ever cease to be a nation before me.'

So we all know that Israel is more and more alive and stronger than ever. I read somewhere it was the fourth military force in the world, which is a lot better than Canada.

It is most likely because of this last verse that so many people tried to destroy Israel, beginning with Rome.

The biggest mistake Louis Riel made, no doubt in my healthy mind I think, was to confide in his friends, priests, bishops and archbishops whom they learned from their master (Paul) that they had to silence such a foolish man and soon was not soon enough. The message I'm talking about can be found in Titus 1, 11. 'Who must be silenced because they are upsetting whole families, teaching things they should not teach for the sake of sordid gain.'

We can see and tell today who has made a sordid gain with their teaching of lies and contradictions. They have million dollars properties in just about every town and village in the world.

So they had to silence Louis Riel one way or the other, because him, just like me won't shut up about the word of God, but this wasn't too easy for the simple reason he had a lot of friends and some of them were very influential. Louis Riel had to flee more than once and this for many years from one end of the country to the other. He also had to flee to the South in the United States and be careful to whom he was talking to, which he didn't always do.

To silence someone, you know what this means, don't you? It is a method well known from the mafia. In my own opinion Paul was not only the first bishop of Rome; he was also one of the first godfather. A lot of them come from Italy.

You see, Louis Riel, like many of us, thought the church's people were God's people. Big mistake! His enemies were everywhere and in big numbers, but fortunately for him, he had a lot of good friends also.

What is better than to let the justice system take care of him? We cannot accuse the court of the Majesty the queen of murder and it's pretty difficult to accuse the government of this crime also. The ones who are guilty of the murder of Jesus of Nazareth and of Louis Riel avoided justice on this earth, but how in the world would they avoid God's justice? Jesus asked God, the Father to forgive his enemies, you would tell me. Yes, and Abraham also asked God, the Father to spare the people of Sodom and Gomorrah, but this didn't stop God from bringing justice over there and to destroyed the bad.

It's a sure thing too that the clergy had a strong influence on the governments in those days. It's easy to understand this when we've learned about what happened in the schools, the boarding schools and in the orphanages.

I can understand why Louis Riel was confused at times, because a lot of what he found in the Bible contradicted everything he learned from the religion and this from when he was a child and he had practically no one to encourage him in his new finding, on the contrary, they look at him as if he was retarded, which contributed, I'm sure in the fits he had from time to time. It's not easy to be accused of mental illness and not to be believed when we are telling the truth, especially the truth which is coming from Jesus and from God. It is a sure thing this is not the nicest thing to happen to a human being. We have to remember then what Jesus said in Matthew 5, 11-12. 'Blessed are you when people insult you, persecute you and falsely say all kinds of evil because of me. (The word of God) Rejoice and be glad, because great is your reward in heaven, for in the same way they persecuted the prophets who were before you.'

Louis Riel knew he had a mission to fulfill coming from God and he couldn't talk to anyone about it without being mocked. I'm sure he had to have a lot of courage to go to the end. I sure can understand him, because I'm going through the same thing. My own brother said I never studied the Bible in my entire life and I live out of his province for more than thirty years. What does he know, really?

I am certain too that Evelina (the priest's sister) whom he loved dearly didn't understand his passion for his mission; otherwise she would have followed him. Although, because of her relationship with the priest and her believes, she would have been a burden to him with his mission, but she didn't and this was the way the Lord wanted it. This also explains to me why the one I love so much didn't want me. God won't allow anything to interfere with my mission either, no matter how much I love her and how pretty and how nice she is. I have to say too that I prayed God not to let her come to me if she wasn't good for me.

According to the story, Louis Riel was so much in love with this woman, (Evelina) that if she had understood him and his mission, he would have come back to get her and they would have been together, at least when their hearts are concerned. On the other hand, if she would have followed him he would have had the clergy on his back a lot sooner, but frankly, I don't think she had the freedom to follow Louis Riel. If she had followed him they would have accused her of mental illness also and locked her up for the rest of her life. So, in one way, it was best for her to stay with her brother, the priest and keep playing the organ for the church. The only fact Louis Riel was in love with this woman proves he was heterosexual. This was enough in itself to get the clergy against him, he who studied to become a priest.

There are one hundred and twenty-five years that separate Louis Riel and I and I know it is technically impossible, but I'm sure he is a man I could have help understand what happened to him. It is possible too that he understood everything himself and the historians or else the members of his surrounding (the priests) on and around his death would have manipulated or even destroyed his documents, his letters and some of his poems that he kept religiously with him, especially the ones that were dangerous for the teaching of the churches. One thing is sure; I don't think the story tells everything that happened concerning the life and the career of Louis Riel.

At his trial he expressed a very strong, almost violent demand to separate from Rome, (the Catholic Church) which contradicts the declaration he was friend with the two priests who were with him at the gallows.

I just know if I was ever to be in this position I would ask for them to get out of my sight and the sooner won't be soon enough. This is said moderately.

It is obvious his papers were scrutinized carefully before the ones that were judged acceptable by the members of the church were given back to his family. Not only the doctor's reports who examined him were screened, but also all of his writing was before it was given to the Prime Minister John A. Macdonald.

If my books ever get censured by the beast I'm sure there will be not much left from them. I let a pastor read my first book one time and I asked him if he liked some of it and he said no. I asked again; not even fifty per cent? And he said; not any. But there is a beautiful love story in it, where the two ended up in heaven with Jesus and God. The book is called; The Precious Princess of Wonderland.

The truth is not welcomed in this world, at least until now. We should know also that a lot of Jesus messages were censured by the beast and disappeared; especially the words that could forbid them to pursue their will to get the business they have today.

I will never believe either that Louis Riel called the two priests; 'Father.' The two priests who were with Louis Riel in the area where his execution took place. Louis Riel was simply too close to Jesus and listened to Jesus too much to do this. He knew what Jesus said in Matthew 23, 9, not to call anyone on earth father and I'm sure also that Louis Riel was faithful to God to his death. The doctors who examined him said in their reports that Louis Riel still when he was on trial had problems with politics and religions. This means that just before his execution Louis Riel still had his mission at heart, no matter what others wanted to make people believe.

He pulled himself away from the priests, the bishops, the archbishops and even from the nuns who betrayed him. Another thing that I'm pretty sure of is he would have never authorized a priest to celebrate the mass over his dead body and if he could stop it he would. He loved God with all his heart, his soul and all of his thoughts and this at least was proven in many places. He understood Jesus' message when Jesus said in Matthew 22, 37-39. 'You shall love the Lord your God with all your heart, and with all your soul, and with all your mind. This is the great and the foremost commandment. The second is like it; you shall love your neighbour as yourself.'

Louis Riel was serving God to the best of his knowledge and he did it to his death; especially because he wasn't afraid to die. He argued against his own lawyers at his trial, no matter the consequences to show he was not alienated; which probably contributed to send him to the gallows and he was aware of it, but the truth was his prime concern, even before his own life. This is why I say that Louis Riel is a hero. If you think he was crazy for this then so was Jesus who gave his own life to bring you the truth that most of the people refuse to this day. I very well know I risk my life too by writing this book, but mainly by publishing it. It is not foolishness, but integrity and love for the truth; which the members of the government and the members of the clergy were lacking and are lacking still today.

It is evident to me that some members of the church with the help of the government changed a lot of facts in the story of Louis Riel by having him to return to the Catholic Church; which he was not anymore and this for the longest time. I have learned from the story of Louis Riel to know that he wasn't catholic anymore and this even just before his death. There was no rosary with him then, just the Lord prayer.

We have to look pretty hard to find the thoughts and the knowledge of Louis Riel, but we don't have to look hard to see that a lot of people wanted to see him dead. I wish I would have had the money to buy his poems which were for sale on the market not too long ago. They were sold for the amount of $26,000.00 in Winnipeg, I heard.

Louis Riel secretary was acquitted because of metal deficiency (a crazy man), but they judged him bright enough to testify in Louis Riel's trial a few days later. He was one of Louis Riel's disciples and he too had problems with politics and religions. They probably thought he was crazy because he too did everything he could to be found guilty. He too understood that there were a lot of things that were not too straight in the Catholic Church's teaching and in Christianity in general. Of course anyone who doesn't think like they do (Christians) are a bit crazy. Did you ever read Chris-ti-an backward? It makes An-ti-Chris. It's pretty amazing, especially after finding what I found; I mean many, many proofs that confirm it.

The similarities between the story of Louis Riel and the story of Jesus are with no dough very obvious. Both of them wanted to save their people. Both of them loved God enough to risk their lives, both of them were mocked, both of them had to flee their enemies to save their lives, both of them were judged, condemned to death and hang to the post. I'm sure too that I could stretch this list quite a bit. I will probably add some more along the way.

Although, the supposedly apostle Paul found the way to say that Jesus and Louis Riel are cursed, because they were hanged to the post and this is most likely why he chose to be dismembered instead of being crucified like it is for roman execution. See Galatians 3, 13. 'Christ redeemed us from the curse of the law (as if the law of God was a curse) by becoming a curse for us, (as if Jesus became a curse) for it is written: 'Cursed is everyone who is hung to a tree.'

I am persuaded too that Louis Riel wanted to spread the word of God to the rest of the world like Jesus did and like

I'm trying to do too for the last fifteen years. I was lucky to understand before it was too late that I have to be careful before I go talk to priests and pastors of the Christians churches, whom proved to me the truth was not always a good thing to tell or rather it was a dangerous thing to tell.

Jesus warned us against the predators, the two legged wolves of this world. Take a look in Matthew 10, 16. 'Behold, I send you out as sheep in the midst of wolves, so be shrewd as serpents and innocent as dove.'

But even being as careful and innocent as you can be, the only fact to talk to anyone about the word of God, I mean the real truth that bothers the churches, especially christian, is a big risk for Jesus' disciples. If you're talking about the truth that contradicts the teaching of the Christian Church to someone who has to protect this institution; don't you expect to be welcome, neither you or the word of God. Beware, it's serious, but it's worth it, because the work for God is never wasted and you can count on God; He won't cheat you like many men would do and there is no one as honest as He is.

I'm still amazed by the fact Louis Riel was followed by such a big number of people, although, I don't think it was because of his knowledge of the word of God in the Bible.

Surely he was one of the rare people who had enough education and on whom the inhabitants of his surrounding could rely on to communicate with the members of the government and understand the craftiness of Sir John A. Macdonald and of the archbishop Taché; who was like his name, which means; stained. One thing is sure; this is Louis Riel was surrounded by many two legs wolves.

Louis Riel was slow taking a wife even though he knew that God wanted him to be fruitful, to multiply and to help fill up the earth.

The fact is the church, the religion, especially the priests don't preach this much this part of the Bible where God said it was not good for a man to be alone. So, Louis Riel most likely found out later than sooner this was the will of God to multiply.

He knew he was a prophet, because he said it himself; which means he knew that the wives of the prophets make young widows and their children become young orphans. He didn't make this statement a lie, because within five years his whole family was gone.

I wouldn't be surprised to learn one day that the wife and the children of Louis Riel didn't live too long after the death of this man because they knew too much about the lies and contradictions that Louis found in the New Testament of the Bible.

I think it might just be the same thing happened to the children of the natives and of the Métis who have been in the residential schools of the West. I found out lately that at least four thousands of them died or never returned home alive.

Although Louis Riel was affected by the influence of the clergy world, priests, bishops, and archbishops and from Paul and company, the one who said it was not good for a man to touch a woman. 1 Corinthians 7, 1, contrary to the word of God, Genesis 2, 18 who said it was not good for a man to be alone. Paul is going even farther when he said wishing that all men be like him. See 1 Corinthians 7, 7, meaning; no women and no children! Maybe he thought he could make the world go on between men alone without women since he likes to do what ever is contrary to God's saying and doing. I know for myself that I would have been very unhappy if I couldn't touch this marvellous thing a woman is. I composed one of my favourite songs on this subject and it goes like this:

The Smell of Roses

Thank You my Lord, thank You my Lord, thank You my Lord.
1-Thank You my Lord for this wonderful smell of roses.
Thank You my Lord for giving me so many things.
Is it for us time of the apotheosis?
It's time for me to say thank You for great blessings.

I know You are the Almighty
You have made this beautiful flower just for me.
She is faded, as You can see.
Only You can bring her back to what she used to be.

We are the seed, the garden of your kingdom.
Your creation made by your hands, your ambition.
Your enemy, yes this despicable phantom
He has faded my nice flower, my companion.

God You blessed us and You told us. Genesis 1, 28!
To be fruitful, to multiply, fill up the earth.
To rule over, birds in the sky,
Fish in the sea and everything upon the earth!

Thank You my Lord for this wonderful smell of roses.
Thank You my Lord for giving me so many things.
Is it for us time of the apotheosis?
It's time for me to say thank You for great blessings.
Thank You my Lord for making me as your likeness.

It is not a priest, a bishop, an archbishop, a cardinal and neither a pope who could make such a beautiful song to my God. If Paul could do it, he would have created the end of the world about two thousands years ago with his plan not to touch a woman. On the other hand, he created many paedophiles and many homosexuals, men who cannot control their own impulses. By doing so he did which are also contrary to the will of God. It is clear now that the churches are in trouble nowadays and it's not over yet with all the lawsuits, because it is written that it will fall the Babylon the great. The attack on the head has started now and the feet have been in shit for quite some times already; it is just that the head tries to keep a lead on the pot, but when the stew is boiling some vapours are escaping.

When all the witnesses will gather together against this beast; it won't be able to hide its sins anymore and all the goods and the gold it has accumulated over the millenniums won't be enough to erase the lies, the murders, the infamy and the scandals of all kinds.

When Louis Riel mentioned wishing to separate from Rome; it was because he didn't want to be associated to such a monster and the monster killed him.

Maybe Louis Riel didn't always know how to identify the messages of Jesus or else he didn't know to whom to go talk to about them or with enough shrewdness, but one thing is sure, God was talking to him. At least I can understand this, because God talks with me every so often and He proves it to me with some messages that can only come from Him. Like God said it Himself in Numbers 12, 6; He said; 'Hear my words, if there is a prophet among you, I, the Lord, shall make Myself known to him in a vision. I shall speak to him in a dream.'

This book I'm writing now is a living proof.

You could bet big that Paul's churches will do everything they can to stop this book of mine from going around the world. Why is it so hard for pagans to believe in the truth? Is it by jealousy or yet by envy maybe that the members of those churches have always refused to believe such prophets? Yet they didn't hesitate to believe in some idiots who said seeing the virgin who was not a virgin anymore when she died. This woman is dead and buried for a long time now; please let her rest in peace bunch of idolaters.

Louis Riel understood this and he didn't have a rosary with him at the gallows; even though he was accompanied by two priests. The prayer Louis said was the; Our Father, just like Jesus taught us to do. We can understand that he couldn't go to his room to pray. See Matthew 6, 6.

That same day was a glorious day for Louis Riel, because he had an answer to his prayer within a few minutes. He was delivered from evil and this even before he had finished to pray. This last prayer from him is another proof he knew the word of God and he followed God until his last breath. And then the truth, the word of God was choked with him and this for another hundred and some year!

Jesus never asked to pray his mother and neither himself. He even asked not to do like pagans and the hypocrites who make all kinds of faces in front of the assemblies and repeat vain prayers. Jesus also asked us to pray for the ones who persecute us and this is why I think Louis Riel tolerated the two priests who were there with him at his execution. I'm tempted to believe too that he didn't have any choice and he would have preferred to have Gabriel Dumont by his side in his last moments. I still wonder why Dumont couldn't deliver him on time. Louis Riel sure has demonstrated to those two priests what it was like to be a child of God. Those two would have loved to bury Riel too, because Jesus said in Matthew 8, 22; 'Let the dead bury the dead.' Meaning let the sinners bury the cadavers. This is surely what they do best, those sinners, burying the dead. According to this verse, Jesus had nothing to do with them, (the dead) and he was in a hurry to go somewhere else. This message also chows that Jesus had nothing to do with the dead and there is nothing we can do for them and to pray for them bothers the spirits including the Spirit of God.

Louis Riel was seen by abbot Fourmond as an antichrist when just about everything the priest was doing is antichrist. I explain myself quickly here. The priest make people call himself father when Jesus, (the Christ) said not to call anyone on earth father. That's antichrist.

Matthew 23, 9, 'Do not call anyone on earth your father; for One is your Father, He who is in heaven.' PS. Jesus was talking to his disciples and his disciples listen to him. For this reason I know Louis Riel didn't call abbot Fourmond father contrary to what it's written in the story.

The priest celebrates the sacrifice of the mass when it is written that God doesn't like the sacrifice. Take a look at Hosea 6, 6. 'For I delight in loyalty rather than sacrifice and in knowledge of God rather than burnt offerings.' Look also in Matthew 12, 7. 'But if you had known what this means; I desire compassion, and not sacrifice, you would not have condemned the innocent.'

Like Louis Riel and Jesus. It is obvious God doesn't like sacrifices and Jesus confirmed it.

The priest asks people to come and confess their sins to him, a man and flesh. Look at Jeremiah 17, 5. 'Thus says the Lord: Cursed is the man who trusts in mankind and makes flesh his strength, and whose heart turns away from the Lord.'

This is not little to say and I didn't invent this, it is there written in the Holy Bible.

The priest prays the Virgin Mary and all the saints (the dead) which is totally and completely pure idolatry on top of asking all his followers to do the same. Did you ever read somewhere where Jesus said; 'Pray me or my mother? He said when you pray, pray the Father who is in heaven.

Take a look again at Exodus 20, 3-4. 'You shall have no other gods before me. You shall not make for yourself an idol, or any likeness of what is in heaven above or on the earth beneath or in the water under the earth (hell).'

God knows they made hundreds of images of the Virgin Mary, of angels, the statues, the crucifix, the medals of saints who are not, because Jesus said that only one was good and he wasn't even talking about himself but about his Father in heaven. I have another song that I like a lot and it's called:

Only One Is Holy

Only, only, only, One is Holy, Holy, Holy.
He is the Almighty.
Funny, funny, funny, so many are called holy.
When Jesus said, that only One is good.

Part spoken

And he wasn't even talking about himself, but about his Father in heaven, whom he loved dearly and served faithfully.

Part sang

Today, today, today, I know about what's holy.
The truth revealed to me.
The truth from Almighty! This was Jesus' delivery.
The true prophet, the one hanged on the wood.

Part spoken

He didn't do it for the money and neither for gold.
He didn't do it for a religion and neither for an empire.

He did it for the Father and for us, whom he loved more than his own life. This was Jesus, the true prophet of God, who was the King of the Jews in the years 30-33 of our times. He was crowned with thorns while he deserved all the best of this world. Follow his word and you will enter the kingdom of heaven while still on earth, because if you do, you will never die. See Matthew 19, 17.

His word which means that God, the Father will hold you from falling into the abomination that causes spiritual death. Be free from the slavery of sins and experience the total happiness. This was Jesus' and is my wish for you.

Part sang

Only, only, only, One is Holy, Holy, Holy.
He is the Almighty.
Funny, funny, funny, so many are called holy.
When Jesus said, that only One is good.
Yes Jesus said that only One is good.

I already talked about the last day of the week and the Sundays; which is contrary to the Law of God which Jesus also confirmed.

When it comes to the communion, everyone knows they give people flattered bread and they keep the wine for themselves. Rome, the Vatican holds the record for the biggest buyer of wine in the world; this is something I read somewhere one day. I'm pretty sure also it holds the record for the vainest repeated prayers.

The bread and the wine was a representation of the body and the blood Jesus was to pour from the hands of his murderers. His teaching is the bread from heaven, the truth, the word of God that was coming from his mouth, the mouth of Louis Riel and from the mouth of all the Jesus' disciples like me that the Paul's churches keep busy trying to shut them up like they did with Jesus and Louis Riel and so many others. I love to eat this bread, the truth, the word of God and this doesn't please everybody, believe me.

When it comes to the abomination that wants to make believe that God the Father, who doesn't like the sacrifice would have Himself sacrificed his one and only son to death; God couldn't commit this abomination as He called it Himself. Go read carefully 2 Kings 16, 3. 'But he walked in the way of the kings of Israel, and even made is son pass through the fire, (killed) according to the abominations of the nations whom the Lord had driven out from the sons of Israel.'

The Lord God would have chased some nations before the people of Israel because they were killing their first sons; God called this an abomination and He would have done the same thing???? Meaning sacrificed his one and only son?????? I don't think so. Open your eyes people; this is what I'm trying to do for you, just like Jesus did.

The priests are still burning incense in their Sunday service or mass. Please read carefully Isaiah 66, 3. 'But whoever sacrifices a bull is like one who kills a man, (a murderer) and whoever offers a lamb, ('The lamb of God who takes away the sin of the world.') is like one who breaks a dog's neck; whoever makes a grain offering is like one who presents pig's blood, and whoever <u>burns memorial incense</u> is like one who worships an idol. They have chosen their own ways, and their souls delight in their <u>abominations</u>.'

God's enemies said that God sacrificed his own son, John 1, 29; ('The lamb of God who takes away the sins of the world.') to save the world and God Himself said that whoever does such a thing is committing an abomination.

You, who is reading these lines, do you really believe that God could have committed this abomination? I don't. Of course, God couldn't have done it.

Just follow my story and you will see before long that they will try to make me look like crazy and if they don't succeed; they will try to kill me, but to me too my body's death will be a deliverance from evil. This in a sense will make no difference to me in a way, because I will continue to be with God. Like Jesus said Matthew 6, 20. 'But store up for yourselves treasures in heaven.'

I found the fine pearl and nobody can take it away from me. See Matthew 13, 44-46. 'The kingdom of heaven is like a treasure hidden in the field, which a man found and hid again; and from joy over it he goes and sells all that he has and buys that field. Again, the kingdom of heaven is like a merchant seeking fine pearls and upon finding one of great value, he went and sold all that he had and bought it.'

I recognized myself in this. I'll sell everything that I own if I have to and I'll publish all of my books and I also hope this will be soon.

It was prophesied also in a form of a warning by Jesus that when will see the abomination mentioned by the prophet Daniel; it would be time to be careful. Read very carefully Matthew 24, 15. 'Therefore, when you see the abomination of desolation, which was spoken of through Daniel the prophet, standing in holy place, (in the Bible) let the reader understand.'

The French Bible is clearer. It said; 'May the reader be careful when he reads.'

So I was very careful and I found all those things which do not please everyone; especially the Christians churches people and I too ask you, who wants to become Jesus' disciples to be careful, because the traps are in the writings of the Bible, just like Jesus said in the parable of the weeds. Be careful to what you're reading, but also to whom you talk to about it. Remember that Jesus said that even members of your own family would give you away and condemn you to death. Matthew 10, 21. 'Brother will betray brother to death, and a father his child and children will rise up against parents and cause them to be put to death.'

I firmly believe this will happen to the people who will talk to the members of their families about the things I am writing in this book, so be careful.

CHAPTER 2

Louis Riel was careful to what he was reading too, because he found a lot of lies and contradictions in the Bible; especially in the New Testament. Those are abominations which caused me desolation and I'm sure it was the same thing for Louis Riel. But as far as I am concerned I don't think he was careful enough to whom he talked to, at least with his friends, priests, bishops and archbishops.

The priests and the pastors of the Christian churches are specialized in deceiving and in hiding the truth. Beware of what you would say in the Bible's studies; especially if you're not with Jesus' disciples, because they won't hesitate to betray you and to give you away. I can tell you that among the four gospels only one evangelist was a Jesus' disciples or an apostles and this was Matthew, the only one who really had something to loose by following Jesus, but he let everything go and he followed Jesus. All he had to do to make a living is sit down and collect money from people. Yes, he was a tax collector, but he found out that he just found a fine pearl. He is also the only one who spoke about the kingdom of heaven. This makes me believe that the other three didn't really know or meet Jesus, but just reported some stories they heard of. I made another song called:

The Kingdom Of Heaven
Have you seen the kingdom of heaven?
If you believe, how come you didn't see it?

Jesus said the devil was a murderer from the beginning; at least this is what it's written in John 8, 44. When we think about all the murders that occurred since the beginning, one has to wonder how many was made in the name of religions. We only have to remember the crusades and the inquisitions, the war where Israel was almost all destroyed by Rome in the years 67 to 73, where one and one half million people died and the 1939-45 war where six more million Jews dies and Hitler was blessed by Rome for doing it. Now we could add to this list the killing of the Métis and Natives children in the residential schools in Canada. This is nothing to be proud of and it is most likely why our governments and the religions are tempted to keep a lid on this story.

We don't really know either how many babies were killed by Rome when they tried to kill Jesus as a new born and this before he could even walk and bring the truth, the word of God to the world.

Hitler told his people the same lie than Paul did when he said that it was the Jews who killed Jesus. It is written in 1 Thessalonians 2, 15, but Jesus in reality was killed by the Roman soldiers. Hitler with this lie convinced his people to follow him in killing six millions Jews and Paul and his disciple John succeeded in spreading the hatred against the Jews through out the world. It's because of this enormous lie that the Jews lived through the retaliation for the longest time and this from almost all the people or nations of the world and it's not over yet. See 1 Thessalonians 2, 14-15 'The Jews who both killed the Lord Jesus and the prophets, they are not pleasing to God, but hostile to all men.'

The truth is exactly the other way around. Israel is God's first born and the enemies of Israel are God's enemies and beware to everyone who attacks Israel. There is no better protection than God's shield. See Exodus 4, 22-23. 'Israel is my <u>firstborn son</u>, and I told you; 'Let my son go, so he may worship me.' '

When Jesus announced his death he said it was the gentiles who were going to kill him and not the Jews. Israel is the people of God and the enemy of Israel is the enemy of God and woe to the one who attacks it. Look and see what is written in Matthew 20, 18-19. 'Behold, we are going up to Jerusalem, and the Son of Man will be delivered to the chief priests and scribes and they will condemn him to death, and they <u>will hand him over</u> to the <u>gentiles</u> to mock and scourge and <u>crucify him</u>.

So, it is not true that Jesus was killed by the Jews. The Jews were executing their wrong doer by stoning like you can see in John 8, 1-8 for the stoning of the adulteress and in Acts 7, 54-58 for the stoning of Stephen.

On the other hand the Romans, the gentiles were executing by crucifixion. Everyone knows how Jesus died; there is no miracle in this. So, it is not true at all that Jesus was killed by the Jews like Paul and his John said he was and the devils like Hitler perpetuated this lie and the Christian churches keep doing.

The John in the gospel of John is oppressive against the Jews and I don't think the John of Jesus would have done this. I'm going to give you a few examples of what I mean when I talk about this John.

John 3, 16, Jesus only son.

Luke 3, 38; 'Adam, son of God.' Now if Jesus is the only one son of God, whose son is Adam? This is according to the Bible, the book that most people say it only tells the truth. One makes the other one a liar. To cover up this lie not very long ago a bishop of the Catholic Church said that Adam and Jesus are one and the same. It's quite clever, crafty to cover one lie by another one, but it's not very honest and far away from integrity.

We all are the children of God when we're doing the will of the Father who is in heaven. See Matthew 12, 50.

See also Deuteronomy 32, 18-19. 'You neglected the Rock who <u>begot</u> you, and forgot the God who gave you birth, the Lord saw this and spurned them because of the provocation of his sons and daughters.'

God has a lot of children and I'm one of his sons too. Yes, God has many children and he didn't need a woman to make Adam and He neither needed to seed a virgin to make Jesus.

Besides, if Jesus is not from the seed of Joseph, down the line from King David; he cannot be the Messiah, the Christ and this is according to all the prophets before him. Whose son was Isaac? Yes, God allowed Sarah to be with child at age ninety, but He didn't sleep with her and neither did the Holy Spirit.

John 8, 42-44, Jesus told them; 'If God were your Father, you would love me, for I proceeded forth and have come from God, for I have not even come on my own initiative, but He sent me. Why do you not understand what I am saying? It is because you cannot hear my word.

You are of your father the devil and you want to do the desires of your father. He was a murderer from the beginning, and does not stand in the truth because there is no truth in him. Whenever he speaks a lie, he speaks from is own nature, for he is a liar and the father of lies.'

This is the typical description of Paul.

Now, what did God send to the world? The answer is; his word through the mouth of Jesus. See Deuteronomy 18, 18.

Now, in the same conversation, John 8, 56, Jesus would have said; 'Your father Abraham rejoiced to see my day, and he saw it and was glad.'

Now here in the same conversation, this Jesus would have said; 'If God were your Father.' And he would have also said; 'If you were the sons of Abraham.' He also said your father is the devil.' And he would also have said your father Abraham???? There is no way the true Jesus, the son of God could have done this.

No, Jesus didn't lied and he didn't make mistakes either, but this story teller is a liar and he got mixed up in his lies. The John of Jesus wouldn't have made Jesus look like a liar and he wouldn't have told some stories as embarrassing as this one either. Jesus told us that we will recognize the tree by its fruits. See Matthew 7, 15-20. I too say; be careful.

There are many other examples to support what I'm saying about this John and among them there would be the fact that the John of Jesus would have talked about the death of his Brother James. The John of Jesus, the apostle would also have talked about the transfiguration of his Master, Jesus, which is an unforgettable miracle. He would also have talked about seeing Peter walking on the waters to go meet Jesus; which is also unforgettable. Besides, the true John and Peter were always together in their mission. You can see this in Acts 4, 1-21. There are also a big number of lies and contradictions in this John's gospel; enough to be careful of what you read. If you can take my advice; erase it from your vocabulary, because it did a lot of harm and confusion to millions of people and it led to the murder of millions of others. If you want to know more about it, find my other book called; The True Face Of The Antichrist.

For sure Louis Riel seemed to be confused at times, but believe me; there were reasons to be too. It is sure too that he couldn't find support among his friends, the priests, bishops and archbishops, because they had to hide the truth as much as they could. They didn't enter this business; which is the church to let guys like Jesus and Louis Riel destroy it. The time was not come yet, but I think it's getting near now. For what I know and knowing that God was always precise with all He did; He will also be precise with what He has yet to do. I think that exactly two thousands years from the death of Jesus on the cross will be a very critical date. The count down might just have been started then with the rupture of the temple curtain from top to bottom. If it's the case; I might just have the chance to see this day while I'm still here on the earth.

Many details according to my calculations make me believe this is the case. To start with we have to look at Daniel; which I believe is the true revelation. Daniel was told by angels when the end time will come. He was told that the end will come in one time, times and half a time. See Daniel 12, 7.

Let's just say that one time is one thousand years, times would be two thousands years and half a time would be five hundred years. Daniel was there five hundred years before Jesus and Jesus was there two thousands years ago. So Daniel was told about the end almost twenty-five hundreds years ago! This almost makes the count. We are getting close to the end of this actual world; I mean the reign of the devil. The reign of Jesus, the reign of the word of God is about to begin. This should happen two thousands thirty-three years after the birth of Jesus. His reign should last one thousands years; which leads us to three thousands five hundred years after the time Daniel was told one time, times, and half a time. So far this is fitting in.

I think the whole process has started with my writing of this book. In about twenty years time, the good will be separated from the bad and the good souls will shine like the sun in the kingdom of their Father and the bad ones will be weeping and gnashing their teeth on their side. See Matthew 13, 42-43.

May the ones who have eyes to look can see and understand!

There is another calculation that adds up pretty good and makes a lot of sense to me and this is the calculation about the week of the creation by God. It is written that God has created the world in six days and He rested on the seventh day, the last day. Now many people know that to God one day is like one thousand years and one thousand years are like one day. We have a few references about this. Look at Psalm 90, 4. 'For a thousand years in Your sight are like yesterday when it passes by.'

My second one comes from Peter, the most considerate of all the apostles and on the faith of whom Jesus built his one and only church. See 2 Peter 3, 8. 'But don't let this one fact escape your notice, beloved, that with the Lord one day is like one thousand years, and a thousand years are like one day.'

It seems to me that Peter wrote this one for me. Then we can at least agree on this one that to God one thousand years are like one day.

So according to the scriptures; I mean from all the prophets who were there before us, Adam was created six thousands years ago, six day for God. God's day of rest is then about to begin since He couldn't really rest for as long as the devil was wandering upon the earth. His rest will start when the devil will be chained for one thousand years. This is written in Revelation 20, 1-2. Jesus too confirmed God is still at work. Look at John 5, 17. 'My Father is working until now, and I myself am working.'

For what I get out of this message is that Jesus tells us the Father who is in heaven didn't take his day of rest yet. Jesus had a good reason to say not to repeat vain prayers. Now, six thousands years could very well be 2190 millions years; meaning 2,190000 days multiplied by 1000 years. This would come in some ways in accordance with the findings of the scientists of nowadays. The knowledge has increased.

Maybe you would say that I asked you to forget about the gospel of this John. This is true and it's also true that I have a good reason for saying so. The fact is I know what Jesus, the word of God said about the wheat and the weeds, the truth and the lies mentioned in Matthew 13, 24-30 and I think the gospel of John is full of weeds and we can hardly find the truth in it, this is why.

The rest of the New Testament is also full of weeds and you have to be very careful when you read. Don't you ever forget what is written in Matthew 24, 15.

One of the first clues that put me on the track of the antichrist was the fact that approximately ninety-five pour cent of the New Testament was written by Paul and company; him who said was blinded by Jesus, the Jesus who spent most of his time opening the eyes of the blinds. It just didn't add up in my mind. I doubt very much Jesus spent time with Paul. And then when I read the doubtful story of Paul carefully; that Jesus would have blinded him; I discovered a few contradictions or lies in it. See Acts 9, 7. 'The men who travelled with him stood speechless, <u>hearing the voice</u> but seeing no one.'

Now go read Acts 22, 9 and you'll see an obvious contradiction. Here the same story is told by the devil, the liar himself. 'And those who were with me <u>saw the light</u> but <u>did not hear</u> the voice of the one who was speaking to me.'

We don't need to be a genius and neither a university student to understand this story is told in one way in one place and totally to the contrary in the other. In one place they heard and saw nothing and in the other they saw the light but heard nothing. The decision is yours to believe or not in the lies, but

I prefer by far to believe in the truth. Now add to this lie or contradiction five hundreds more and you too will understand who is the antichrist and why I reacted the way I did.

According to 1 John 4, 3, the brother of Jesus, the antichrist was already in the world in the time of Jesus. If you really want to know who makes people blind, go read Acts 13, 10-11. Paul said. 'You who are full of all deceit and fraud, you son of the devil, you enemy of all righteousness, will you not cease to make crooked the straight ways of the Lord?

Now behold, the hand of the Lord is upon you and <u>you will be blind</u> and not see the sun for a time. And immediately a mist and a darkness fell upon him and he went about seeking those who would lead him by the hand.'

It did cross my mind that Paul was telling his own story here, I mean, the story of his encounter with Jesus. See Acts 9, 7-9.

I know for what I read, when the hand of Jesus was on somebody this person was healed immediately.

Paul made this man blind apparently, but I know he blinded billions others with his lies and contradictions. The devil too is powerful, but he is mainly mean, seducer and crafty.

But believe me; Jesus didn't make anyone blind, on the contrary; he opens the eyes of the blinds and he does it with the word of God. Take my word for it or take the word of God. Jesus didn't come to judge or to punish and neither to condemn but he came to teach us, to deliver us from evil and to save us from death, meaning from sins. 'Go and sin no more.' He said many times. The only way he can do it, it's for us to repent, to turn to God and to stay away from sin. This is the main message from God.

Paul on the contrary; him a murderer who never did repent. See 1 Corinthians 4, 4. 'For I am conscious of nothing against myself.'

He made people blind, he judged people, he sword many times and punished people contrary to the teaching of Jesus, he is responsible for the killing of many Jesus' disciples and he felt guilty of nothing and all this after his supposedly conversion to Jesus.

See what Jesus said in Matthew 7, 1-2. 'Do not judge so that you will not be judge. For in the way you judge, you will be judge and by your standard of measure it will be measured to you.'

See Paul in 1 Corinthians 6, 2-3. 'Or do you not know that the saints will judge the world? If the world is judge by you, are you not competent to constitute the smallest law courts? Do you not know that we will judge the angels? How much more matters of this life?'

Not only Paul was judging others, but he was also teaching his disciples to do the same. Not only Paul was judging people, contrary to the will of God, but he didn't waste any time before judging the angels of heaven also.

See now 1 Galatians 1, 8-9. 'But even if we or <u>an angel from heaven</u> should preach a gospel other than the one we preached to you, let him be eternally condemned! As we have already said, so now I (Paul) say again, if anybody is preaching to you a gospel other than what you accepted, (full of lies and contradictions) let him be eternally condemned.'

Men, if this is not the devil himself, he's got to be his right arm. Could this be him (Paul) who said not to curse? He condemned even an angel of heaven. Not only he blasphemed but he repeated his blasphemy. It seems to me the guy likes to send people to hell and this is not enough for him, he tried to send God's angels too. He's not talking about a hell angel here, but an angel from heaven and Paul's gospels are totally contrary to what Jesus preached.

Take a look now of how Paul judged others. 1 Timothy 5, 24. 'The sins of some men are quite evident even before we judge them.'

See also Romans 3, 4. 'So you triumph when you judge.'

See Paul again in 1 Corinthians 5, 3. 'For I, on my part, though absent in body but present in spirit, have already judged him who have so committed this, as though I was present.'

There we are, the spirit who was to come is in the picture. Only in John gospel we can see the helper that Jesus will send over. In French the helper is not mentioned, but the word is Counselor. But no where else it is mentioned than in John 14, 16, 14, 26, 15, 26, 16, 7 and 16, 13 except in Job 29, 25. This is where Paul was introduced. See now 1 Corinthians 4, 3-4. 'But to me it is a very small thing that I may be judged by you or by any human court; in fact, I do not judge myself. For I am conscious of nothing against myself.'

The spirit has spoken. This man was arresting and killing the Jesus' disciples, but of course if there is no law for him, there is no sin.

See 1 Corinthians 11, 31. 'But if we judge ourselves rightly, we would not be judged.'

See Acts 23, 2-3. The high priest Ananias commanded those standing beside him (Paul) to strike him on the mouth. Then Paul said to him, 'God is going to strike you whitewashed wall! Do you sit to try me according to the Law, and in violation of the Law order me to be struck?'

I think Paul was talking about the Roman law; it was extremely dangerous for a Jew to strike a Roman in those days. He just said it didn't matter to him to be judged by anyone or any human court. What it would have been if this was important to him? The Roman soldiers would have destroyed the court and the judge. This is most likely what happened. Paul knew they were outside just waiting for a signal and they were there to protect any Roman against any Israel court.

Paul called the high priest whitewashed wall and I'm pretty sure this wasn't too flattering. These are the same men he called his brothers in many places in the Bible.

Please read now Matthew 5, 22. 'But I say to you that every one who is angry with his brother shall be guilty before the court; and who ever say to his brother, you good for nothing, should be guilty before the high court; and who ever says, you fool, shall be guilty enough to go into the fiery hell.'

So according to these words from Jesus Paul deserved to be judged by the court; he deserved to be before the high court and he deserved to go in the fiery hell, because he was angry with his brother, he called his brother whitewashed wall, which is just as bad as fool, this is not too good coming from a so called apostle, him Paul, who wished that all men be like he is, to be his imitators. Please God, keep this man, this Paul and his teaching far away from me?

Some of you would probably say; 'Yes, but the high priest was not Paul's brother.' Then go read carefully Acts 23, 1. 'Paul, looking intently at the council, said, '<u>Brethren</u>, I have lived my life with a perfectly good conscience before God up to this day.'

So for Paul having arrested and killed the disciples of Jesus didn't bother his conscience one little bit; even after he supposedly became an apostle converted to Jesus and this from his own testimony. Open your eyes, would you people for Jesus sake?

Jesus said another one will come in his own name and they will receive him. See John 5, 43. Many didn't understand yet this other one is Paul who is now received by almost all Christians in the world and he lies and he condemns, he swears and judges, he is a hypocrite, he ran people down, he pretends to be a father without touching a woman, he called people's names, he blasphemed, he contradicts Jesus, God and himself, he brags, he fights with the ones he calls his brothers, he made people blind in more than one way, he changed the Law of God, he preaches about himself rather than about Jesus of Nazareth, he has circumcised Timothy after condemning the circumcision and is there a person more arrogant than he is? See Genesis 17, 13, an everlasting covenant between God and mankind. Paul did all of this after his conversion to Jesus. Before all of this he was killing the Jesus' disciples. And after all this his conscience is totally clear and he never repented of anything and this according to himself. It is a fact that the devil is way too proud to repent.

How could we believe that Jesus would have chosen a disciple or an apostle to do and say so many things contrary to what he taught his apostles and to put some spokes in the apostles wheels and to throw a spanner in their works? No way.

Some people would say that I put Paul down too. What ever I do is to open your eyes and not to shut them up like Paul did, because I like the truth and I'm very sorry to see there are so many blinds in the world.

Paul Swears

Swearing is to take God as a witness of what we say or do.

What is following is something the liars use a lot, but Jesus' disciples don't; simply because Jesus asked us not to do it.

See Paul in 2 Corinthians 1, 23. 'But I call God as a witness to my soul, that to spare you I did not come again to Corinth.'

I agree on one thing here; if Paul didn't return over there the Corinthians were spared alright.

See also Romans 1, 9, 2 Corinthians 11, 31, Philippians 1, 8, 1 Timothy 5, 2, 2 Timothy 4, 1 to see how Paul swears.

See too what Jesus said about swearing in Matthew 5, 34-37. 'But I (Jesus) say to you, make no oath at all, either by heaven, for it is the throne of God, or by the earth, for it is the footstool of his feet, or by Jerusalem, for it is the city of the great King. Nor shall you make an oath by your head, for you cannot make one hair white or black. But let your statement be yes, yes, or no, no, anything beyond these is of evil.'

This is from the devil. I'm not the first one to say that governments, our courts of justice, police force and armies are antichrist. And one more time Jesus showed me who is the devil. No one and no statement can be any clearer. Now you know the definition of swearing and to do it is antichrist. Does it start to click in now?

PAUL A HYPOCRITE

See Acts 23, 4-5. 'But the bystanders said; 'Do you revile God's high priest?' And Paul said, 'I was not aware, <u>brethren</u> that he was high priest, for it is written; 'You shall not speak evil of a ruler of your people.'

The hypocrite; he was working for them.

Look at Acts 26, 10. 'And this is just what I did in Jerusalem; not only I lock up many of the saints in prisons, <u>having received authority from the chief priests</u>, but also when they were being put to death, I cast my vote against them.'

I recognized the tree by its fruits! Thanks to you Jesus.

And from here all the way to Rome Paul saved his head by telling the same story that he chased all the way to the foreign cities, that he arrested, put them in prisons and killed the Jesus' disciples.

Take a look too at Acts 26, 12. 'While so engaged as I was journeying to Damascus <u>with the authority and commission of the chief priests</u>.'

See Acts 22, 4-5. 'I persecuted this Way to the death, binding and putting both men and women into prisons, as also the <u>high priest</u> and all the council of the elders can testify. <u>From them I also received letters</u> to the brethren and started off to Damascus in order to bring even those who were there in Jerusalem as prisoners to be punished.'

Can you see that the high priests were Paul's brothers and so were the Damascus brothers. Ananias from Damascus, the so called disciple was one of them too. See Acts 9, 10-19.

In Acts 9, 20 Paul had started already to disobey Jesus. 'And immediately he began to proclaim Jesus <u>in the synagogues</u>, saying, 'He is the son of God.'

Look at Matthew 10, 1-17. Jesus told his apostles to enter some deserving houses and that we will be scourged in the synagogues. It is clear to me that Jesus wanted his disciples to stay away from the synagogues. Besides, the Jews wouldn't let

Paul and no one else preaching in their synagogues in those days; especially not to say that Jesus was the son of God. See John 19, 7. 'The Jews answered him, 'We have a law and by that law he ought to die because he made himself out to be the son of God.'

Wasn't it him, Paul who accused Peter to be a hypocrite? See Galatians 2, 11-16.

Do you understand now that there was nothing in the world that could please more the Pharisees, the Sadducees, the kings and all the leaders all the way from Jerusalem to Rome? For them to hear that one of their own (Paul) was destroying the enemy of Rome was exceptional. He is crafty the devil and Paul too. All of this happened after the so called conversion of Paul to Jesus.

Paul made it to Rome saving his life by telling who ever wanted to hear it that he persecuted to death the Jesus' disciples. This was quite a way to be an apostle. Telling the truth that it is on this man, this Paul and his teaching that the Christian Churches were founded makes me a target just like Jesus and Louis Riel! If you can count all the Christians or I should say all the ones who believe that the Bible is the absolute truth; then you can almost count all my enemies. Read Matthew 10, 34. 'Do not think that I came to bring peace on the earth; I did not come to bring peace, but a sword.'

The two edges sword is the truth, the word of God and if it causes divisions; it's because some people believe in it and others don't. Some people accept the truth and others reject it.

Now, please let me translate Matthew 10 verse 37 in English for you from my point of view. 'Who ever loves his father or mother more than the word of God is not worthy of the word of God and who ever loves his son or daughter more than the word of God is not worthy of the word of God.'

The same thing goes for Matthew 19, 14. 'Leave the little children come to the word of God, for the kingdom of heaven belongs to such as them.'

I just wonder how many people love their artistic and sport idols and their religion more than the word of God. I just know they are a lot. Just like Jesus said it, it is not peace in my family either. Not too many of my closed ones are ready to accept the truth, but for most of them it's not because of the idols, but mostly because of their religion which became more or less their god. They were kind of brainwashed by the lies from their spiritual fathers, their leaders.

For sure Louis Riel was not spared from this plague either. There are a few clues that he went through this too. To say that Jesus and his disciples and people like Louis Riel risked their lives and died to light up people who most of the time didn't want to see and neither hear about the truth; it is almost discouraging. I just hope God will give me the strength to make it to the end; not only for somebody else salvation, but for mine too.

See Matthew 10, 22. 'You will be hated by all because of my name, (the word of God) but it is the one who endured to the end who will be saved.'

See also Matthew 24, 12-13. 'Because lawlessness is increased, most people's love will grow cold, but the one who endures to the end, he will be saved.'

Here is what I would like to add to this statement. You will be hated by all who don't love God.

This is what Jesus did; persevere to the end and I truly believe this is what Louis Riel did too; contrary to what the priests around him wanted to let people think; meaning that Louis Riel died as a Catholic.

I will never believe this unless Louis Riel tells me himself that he turned away from his mission just before he died. He proved many times he wasn't afraid to die before the crucial last moment. One of the proofs is the fact Louis Riel prayed our Father who is in heaven then and he had no rosary with him.

When it comes to the lawlessness and the love of the most being cold off; this is already here. I won't be surprised nowadays if God would have a hard time finding a young virgin of fourteen years of age, but on the other hand He wouldn't have trouble at all finding a man of sixty to get her pregnant.

Catholic in French which is catholique and according to the value of the letters the name makes the number of the beast, the 666 and I'll explain this to you right away for the ones who don't know what it is. The value of the letters is read this way; a = 6, b = 12, c = 18 and this straight to the end of the alphabet.

C = 18
A = 06
T = 120
H = 48
O = 90
L = 72
I = 54
Q = 102
U = 126
E = 30

Total 666, the number of the beast, but catholic is not the beast, but just a member of it, the head maybe. The beast is quite more powerful than the Catholic Church. Although, the Catholic Church is quite powerful itself and it did prove it over the years.

When it was prophesied that the love of the most will cool off we weren't told a precise date, but no later than yesterday we got the proof of this phenomenal event on the news. On April 26, 2010 on a sidewalk of the town of New York a man who just saved the life of another person was stabbed and lay down bleeding to death while twenty-five people passed by him without bothering calling for help or calling the police or an ambulance or even tried to help him. One person out of twenty-six finally called for help. Four per cent of the town of eight point three millions! Three hundred thirty-two thousand people out of more than eight millions are not totally cold off yet and this according to the calculations of the surveys of nowadays with five per cent chance of error, one out of twenty.

Let me tell you that this one person who died that day on the sidewalk has way more luck than the other twenty-five who didn't bother with him.

I have to say that the town of New York is not an easy place to live. I visited it in 1981 and I saw from my own eyes in three different places men lying on the sidewalk too drunk to get up and when I wanted to see if I could help I was told to stay away from them if I didn't want to be stabbed. On the other hand, to see a person dying on a sidewalk without calling for help is cowardice pure and simple.

Chapter 3

To stay, sort of speech with the calculation; we know that computer also makes the number of the beast and no one can truly say this is not an important tool for the system to find predators.

C = 18
O = 90
M = 78
P = 96
U = 126
T = 120
E = 30
R = 108

Tot.666, but as I already said; the computer is only a tool the beast though wouldn't hesitate to use to find the ones who have the mark of the beast and mainly the ones who don't have it.

When this day comes we would have to flee just like Noah had to when the flood started and like Lot and his family had to flee too when God had enough with the degeneration of Sodom and Gomorrah. With all the adultery, the abortions, the idolatry, the gay marriages, the killing and the murders, the fornication that goes around in the world nowadays and I can't name them all; there are too many; we are not too far from God's anger one more time.

See Psalm 86, 15. 'But You O Lord are a God merciful and gracious, slow to anger and abundant in loving, kindness and truth.'

Don't fool yourselves; He is rich in justice too.

Jesus has worn us many times. See Matthew 24, 20. 'But pray that your flight will not be in winter or on a Sabbath.'

See also Matthew 10, 23. 'But when ever they persecute you in one city, flee to the next.'

This is something Louis Riel had to do many times.

See Matthew 24, 18. 'Who ever is in the field must not turn back to get his cloak.'

The warnings are there and we just have to be ready when the time comes and don't you think it is a last minute duty. Just remember that God doesn't like hypocrisy. Remember too that Noah was laughed at and mocked and so were Lot, Jesus, Louis Riel and I will be too. It is one thing to know we'll have to flee, but we still have to know where to go and what to do.

You must know by now that I'm not too bad with numbers. There is another calculation I made following another one of Jesus' message who said this. See Matthew 22, 14. 'Many are called, but few are chosen.'

See also Matthew 7, 14. 'For the gate is small and the way is narrow that leads to life and there are few who fin it.'

This means that when Jesus, the truth, the word of God would have separated the few chosen sheep (the good) from the big number of goats (the bad) who would be thrown in the fiery furnace where there will be weeping and gnashing of teeth; there will be just a few chosen ones to reign over; unless the good souls from the beginning of the world are resurrected like some of the prophets said it longtime ago.

Read in Ezekiel 37, 1-14. 'The hand of the Lord was upon me, and he brought me out by the Spirit of the Lord and set me down in the middle of the valley; and it was full of bones. He caused me to pass among them round about, and behold, there were very many on the surface of the valley, and lo, they were very dry. He said to me; 'Son of Man, (which means prophet just like Jesus) can these bones live?' And I answered, 'O Lord God, You know.' Again He said to me; 'Prophesy over these bones and say to them; 'O dry bones, hear the word of the Lord." "Thus says the Lord God to these bones; 'Behold, I will cause breath to enter you that you may come to life. I will put sinews on you, make flesh grow back on you, cover you with skin and put breath in you that you may come alive; and you will know that I am the Lord.'

So I prophesied as I was commanded, and as I prophesied, there was a noise, and behold, a rattling, and the bones came together, bone to its bones. And I looked, and behold, sinews were on them, and flesh grew and skin covered them; but there was no breath in them. Then he said to me, 'Prophesy to the breath, prophesy, Son of Man, and say to the breath, thus says the Lord God; 'Come from the four winds, O breath, and breathe on these slain, that they come to life.' So I prophesied as He commanded me, and the breath came into them, and they came to life and stood on their feet, an exceedingly great army. Then He said to me; 'Son of Man, these bones are the whole house of Israel; behold, they say; 'Our bones are dried up and our hope has perished. We are completely cut off.' 'Therefore prophesy and say to them; 'Thus says the Lord God; 'Behold, I will open your graves and cause you to come up out of your graves, my people; and I will bring you into the land of Israel. Then you will know that I am the Lord, when I have opened your graves and cause you to come up out of your graves, my people.

I will put my Spirit within you and you will come to life, and I will put you on your own land. Then you will know that I, the Lord, have spoken and done it declares the Lord.'

This was a bit long, but I thought it was an important message. We can find more about it in Matthew 25, 46. 'These will go away into eternal punishment, but the righteous to eternal life.'

See also Daniel 12, 2. 'Many of those who sleep in the dust of the ground will awake, these to everlasting life, but the others to everlasting contempt.'

This is the word of God, don't be fool. See too John 5, 29. 'These who did the good deeds to resurrection of life, those who committed the evil deeds to resurrection of judgement.'

What is missing in this last phrase here is without repentance. I also think it is time for another song, which I called;

On Which Side Are You?

Would you be on the side of Jesus?
Would you be with the one who has done?
The ultimate sacrifice,
He's the one who paid the price
So you can get to the truth
Which has hidden from you his enemy.
Would you be on the side of Jesus?
Would you look to what he has done?
For us he listened to God,
And for us he poured his blood
The bad ones were happy;
Would you be too like his enemy?
Would you be on the side of Jesus?
Would you be with the one who has done?
Who has made us the promise
That we will see liveliness.
When we will be accused and
Sometime confused by the enemy.
Would you be on the side of Jesus?
Would you be with the one who has done?
Telling us to be shrewd
When the beast will be rude
When we'll be persecuted and
We will have to flee the enemy.
Would you be on the side of Jesus?
Would be with the one who has done?
When he'll come back to get us,
The ones who have carried their cross
We will be on his right side and

On the other side his enemies.
I know I am on the side of Jesus.
Yes I am on the side of the one
Who has told me all the truth and
I recognized the fruit
And for sure we will win,
Jesus said on his enemy.
Yes I am on the side of Jesus.

You who are reading these pages, do you know on which side you are? If you're not on God's side while you are on earth; you cannot expect to be with God when you reach the other side and only you can decide your destiny. You better think seriously about it.

When they asked Jesus if he was really the king of the Jews he answered; see Matthew 27, 11. 'You said it.'

There were two important things for a man to become the King of Israel. The first thing he needed to be is a direct descendant of King David which Jesus was; only if he was the biologic son of Joseph, his father. See Luke 1, 31-33. 'Behold, you will conceive in your womb and bear a son and you shall call him Jesus. He will be great and will be called the son of the Most High and the Lord God will give him the throne of <u>his father David</u>; and he will reign over the house of Jacob forever and his kingdom will have no end.'

This is another proof that Jesus is a Son of Man, a prophet who became the son of God when he gave up everything to consecrate his life to do the will of God. It was at that time God said; see Matthew 3, 17. 'And behold, a voice out of heavens said, 'This is my son in whom I am well-pleased.' '

Another important thing Jesus needed to be the King of Israel was to be anointed and this is what happened at Jesus' baptism. Jesus was and is a real King of Israel as a man, as a human even though God is the King of kings and King of all the earth.

It is written that the truth would set you free. See Psalm 72, 14. 'He will rescue their life from oppression and violence.'

I would like to translate this in my own way, with my own words. He will set me free from evil, from the slavery of religions. In my case Jesus is victorious and I'm very grateful to him. Thank You O my Lord for this.

Jesus said the prostitutes and the publicans will enter the kingdom of heaven before the scribes and the Pharisees. Let me tell you they will enter before any leader of any religion too; especially the Christian ones. I can tell you that I talked to many of these leaders and to many Christian people who rejected me with my word of God, but the few prostitutes to whom I talked to did listen to what I had to say and not only they understood, but they also accepted the word of God. They won't lose their reward, word of God, see Matthew 10, 42.

In general most of the people who are not attached to a church or to a religion are more willing to receive the word of God. This is kind of strange I think. This was for me a very little calculation to make; it is just that the ones who don't go to church too often are not brainwashed as bad as the ones who keep going.

I challenge anyone to take any of my messages from this book of mine and mention it to any priest or pastor, father of your congregation and you'll be advised not to touch this book anymore, you will be advised to destroy it and to stay as far as possible from anything that touches me. Do you see, the word of God, the truth could be contagious?

There is another thing I suggest you to do if you go to church and this is to note what is said in every sermon on Sunday morning from your father. You'll find out very soon they preach Paul at ninety per cent and Jesus just enough to make you believe they are preaching the truth. You will never hear a priest preach Matthew 23, 9. 'Do not call anyone on earth your father; for only one is your Father, He who is in heaven.'

Did you ever hear a preacher talk about Leviticus 18, 22. 'You shall not lie with a male as one lies with a female; it is an abomination.'

Not too many people preach against themselves. Now this abomination is all over. How could a preacher who is a paedophile or a homosexual speak about this or against this; especially if his condition is known from his congregation?

It is almost impossible nowadays to turn on the TV without seeing one of them one way or the other. It's getting to be disgusting. I wish we could put them all in a reserve apart from others to avoid this pandemic. Not too many priests preach Matthew 3, 11 either. 'As for me, (John the Baptist) I baptize you with water for repentance, but he who is coming after me is mightier than I, and I am not fit to remove his sandals; he will baptize you with the Holy Spirit and fire.'

The baptism Jesus gave to his disciples is the truth, the word of God.

This only means one thing and this is the water baptism is over or should be over since Jesus came; at least for people who follow Jesus anyway. This means the newborn babies baptism is not coming from God and doesn't bring babies to God either.

Jesus spent three years of his life teaching his disciples; risking his life almost continually to get people free from the slavery of the religions. 'The truth will set you free.' Jesus didn't baptize with water either.

Matthew 10, 17. 'But beware of men, for they will hand you over to the courts and scourge you in their synagogues.'

This is a message to the Jesus' disciples to stay away from Judaism. Then with everything I already mentioned about the catholic religion, father, confession, baptism, communion, prayers, idolatry and a lot more; there are many proofs this religion is antichrist.

Antichrist is a word which is intriguing me a bit more than others. If you read Christian backward; I mean starting with the last syllable; this will give you; an ti Christ. For some strange reason in French they choose to change the word antichrist for antéchrist. They changed the vowel I for an E and Christian in French is chrétien; which doesn't contain the word Christ like it does in English.

The word chrétien seems to come from believing rather than from Christ. I personally think this was done on purpose to fool the world; to make it a bit harder for people to find the name of the beast; which number is six, six, six. I also think the Catholic Church had and still have a huge influence on the way to write words; especially about what concerns this church. See Revelation 13, 18. 'Here is wisdom. Let him who has understanding <u>calculate</u> the number of the beast, for the number is that of a man, and his number is six hundred and sixty-six.'

I don't think I am wiser or more intelligent than anyone else, but on the other hand I listen to my God who told me through Jesus to be shrewd like a serpent and simple like a dove.

If you want to be killed quickly you just have to find the name of the beast and go tell your father at your church. I found this name of the beast which was carefully hidden behind a single vowel, an I for an E in chrétienté, which means (Christianity). A Jesus' disciple, a person from God wouldn't have challenge the world to find the name of the beast, but he would have worn the world population of who the beast was or is. This is not a matter to play the mice and cat game; it is way too serious. The most disgusting of all is it's the creator of this beast who challenged the world to find his name. He's got some nerves this devil. The name is Italian just like this devil and I have all the necessary proofs I need to back me up. I only need to find out how long I'll survive now after this book is published. For sure if someone else found it and talked about it, he was eliminated.

C =   18
H =   48
R =   08
I =   54
T = 120
I =   54
E =   30
N =   84
T = 120
<u>É =   30</u>

Tot.= 666. Here it is the name of the beast and believe me; this beast is very powerful and has proven in the pass it wasn't shy about killing the ones who troubled it. I know for myself its reign is getting close to its end either it kills me or not. This book is from God and is in God's hands and will survive me. This beast is quite silly though, because even the members of the beast have been looking to find his name for years and the least I can say is they will look very silly when they find out what it is.

The witnesses of.....J; the ones who pretend to be God's witnesses among others take the name of God in vain in the face of the world; breaking this way the God's second commandment. By doing so, I mean by using God's name; not only they break the second commandment, but they make others break it too when they talk about them ether good or bad.

Even Jesus didn't dare pronouncing the name of God and he referred to Him with the words; 'My Father who is in heaven.' Although I think the most dangerous religion is the Baptist evangelist, because it looks more than any others like an angel of light. Take a look at 2 Corinthians 11, 14. 'No wonder, for even Satan disguises himself as an angel of light.'

Believe Paul on this one; he knows it.

There are numerous proofs that Paul is the creator of the Christian religions and it is obvious that Jesus was against this. Paul is also probably responsible for all the religions born since the death of Jesus.

Everything the devil could do to contradict Jesus and God he did it. It's Paul who created the seven churches that you can read about in the New Testament and in revelation. It's Paul who is the mortal enemy of Jesus and of everything which is called saint. Louis Riel understood this and this is why they had to kill him. See Matthew 13, 39. 'And the enemy, who sowed them (lies), is the devil.'

This was the main reason why Louis Riel asked to be separated from Rome. God loves me a lot too; to allow me to separate from Rome, from the Catholic Church some forty-eight years ago. Many unpleasant events allowed me to open my eyes; things like a priest who practically stole our house I worked very hard to build it. The same priest who used this house to shelter his mistresses; which his own daughter inherited at his death. When all of their crimes and their scandals come up at the time of the judgement; it will not look too good for the enemies of God! For sure there will be weeping and gnashing of teeth.

Le Judgement

Can we only imagine the time it would take to judge everyone and from all the nations and from all the generations from the beginning of the world if we weren't judged at the death of everyone of us? Fortunately and Jesus said it that all the names of the ones who are saved are already written in the book of life. I can just imagine what the sons of the devil will do when Jesus tells me; 'You who are blessed by my Father come to sit at my right.'

The sons of the evil one would stand like a crown lawyer to say; 'He was sexually obsessed, he was a liar like everyone of us, he abandoned his wife and children, he didn't always pay his debts, he didn't always respect his parents, he persecuted our churches. We cannot tell he loved his brother, he acted improperly towards his sisters, he stole, little, but he did, he swore like everybody else, he masturbated and wasted the seed of life, he fought with others more often than on his own turn, he was not summitted to the authorities.'

The Great Judge then will ask the devil; 'Would you be done soon?' But the devil will want to continue his accusations. Then the Judge will say: 'I don't remember any of all this.'

Then the sons of the devil will come in big numbers with more accusations even more incriminating. 'You said if a man committed adultery in his heart he is guilty of adultery; so he's guilty of this too and if he has committed murder in his heart he is a murderer; so this man is guilty of murder too.'

The Judge will tell him one more time: 'I don't remember any of this.'

Then the devil will get real mad and accuse God to be impartial and unfair. God will give him a slap that will send the devil away for a long distance, but this devil is very stubborn and obstinate and he wouldn't give up this easy and come viciously back on the attack. "He distressed the entire world by decapitating the Holy Bible like no one did before him."

Then the Great Judge will tell him: "It's Me who asked him to do it because you put way too many lies in it and this to deceive my people." "But it is written in revelation 22, 19 that if anyone takes away from the words of the book of this prophesy You will take away his part from the tree of life and from the holy city; which is written in this book." "You know very well that it's not Me who condemned before the judgement; you did it and because you are a liar from the beginning and that you and your sons never repented for your sins; you will never have the right to the eternal life, but you will have the right to the eternal shame. The accused here present repented for all of his sins and this is why I don't remember any of them according to My Word. I forgot everything he could have done wrong from the time he was born. He believes in Me and he listened to my word. He loves Me and contrary to you; he hates evil and he loves the truth. So he will take his place that belongs to him in my kingdom."

Then we will have dances and singing of joy on the righteous side and there will be weeping and gnashing of teeth on the evil side. I can just imaging how it would be if God remembers everything we have done wrong if we didn't repent. He would have no other choice than to tell the devil he is right and to tell those lost souls; see Matthew 25, 41. 'Depart from Me, accused ones, into the eternal fire which has been prepared for the devil and his angels.'

When Jesus started his ministry he was saying, see Matthew 4, 17. 'From that time Jesus began to preach and say, 'Repent for the kingdom of heaven is at hand.' '

The kingdom of heaven is at hand alright, because you can enter it as soon as you have sincerely repented of all your sins.

If only listening to these words is for us the only chance to be saved many people screwed it up. Many ignored it or else traded it for this one which was never said by Jesus, but by Paul in Ephesians 5, 2. 'And walk in love, just as Christ also loved you and gave himself up for us, an offering and a sacrifice to God as a fragrant aroma.'

You have to see again Isaiah 1, 11.

Now see what happens if you compare this last verse from Paul to another one of Paul in 1 Corinthians 10, 20. See what you get. 'But I say that the things that we sacrifice, we sacrifice to demons and not to God.'

So according to this last statement from Paul and what it is written in John 3, 16; God would have sacrificed his only son, Jesus to the demons. This is from Paul, the kind of apostle that billions of Christians in the world believe in?????????

Jesus gave himself alright, but he didn't give himself to die but to instruct us about the word of God, the way to heaven, the way to be saved and the truth is he doesn't save us with his death, but he saves us with the truth, with his knowledge, with the world of God. Listen to him and believe him. See what God said to Isaiah in Isaiah 53, 11. 'By his knowledge my righteous <u>servant</u> will justify many.'

I also think Paul sacrificed himself to demons. He certainly taught a lot of devilish things and contrary to the teaching of Jesus. Paul was swearing, judging, cursing, blaspheming, slandering, and mainly condemning many people to hell and handing others over to Satan.

Here are a few examples of this. See 1 Timothy 1, 20. 'Among these are Hymenaeus and Alexander, whom I have handed over to Satan.'

See also 1 Corinthians 5, 5. 'I have decided to deliver such a one to Satan.'

The least we can say is Paul had a very strange way to save people and I don't think he learned this from Jesus at all. Here is what God said in Jeremiah 31, 34. 'For I will forgive their iniquity and their sins, I will remember no more.'

See also Isaiah 45, 25. 'In the Lord all the offspring of Israel will be justified and will glory.'

So it is very clear that the sincere repentance is the key of salvation and this is the reason why Jesus suffered and died to make us understand. It is for the same reason that all the disciples and all the Jesus' apostles suffered and still suffer trying to open your eyes on this subject. Please don't make all their efforts and their courage being in vain.

Don't forget that once you sincerely repented your sins are forgotten and erased; so please stop confessing your sins again and again once you repented. Don't remind God of them, because He doesn't want to remember them anymore. People who do are lacking faith and don't believe in God enough to believe Him.

There was a good reason why Jesus told us not to repeat vain prayers. See Matthew 6, 7. 'And when you are praying, do not use meaningless repetition as the Gentiles do (Romans, Catholics, Christians with their rosary) for they suppose that they will be heard for their many words.'

The repentance has everything to do with the <u>kingdom of heaven</u> and Jesus talked about it quite often. We can find these three words in Matthew and in Matthew only. Why, would you ask me? I would say that Matthew is the only one apostle among the four evangelists who lived and followed Jesus when it comes to the gospels. Luke was a very close friend of Paul until death tore them apart. See 2 Timothy 4, 11. 'Only Luke is with me. Pick up <u>Mark</u> and bring him with you.'

I think it would be good for me now to make a few comparisons.

See Matthew 19, 14. 'But Jesus said: 'Let the children alone and do not hinder them from coming to me, (the word of God) for the <u>kingdom of heaven</u> belongs to such as these.' '

Mark 10, 14. 'But when Jesus saw this, he was indignant and said to them, 'Permit the children to come to me, do not hinder them, for the <u>kingdom of God</u> belongs to such as these.' '

Luke 18, 16. 'But Jesus called for them, saying, 'Permit the children to come to me, do not hinder them, for the <u>kingdom of God</u> belongs to such as these.' '

Luke and Mark never followed Jesus, but Matthew did it and this John of John's gospel never heard these words from Jesus either. On the other hand the John that Jesus chose did, but we don't have much from him.

So, do you see that the kingdom of heaven and the kingdom of God are two different places and two different eras? The kingdom of God will take place at the end of all times while the kingdom of heaven is the kingdom of the ones who choose to live outside the world; meaning outside the kingdom of the devil. We can find the kingdom of heaven thirty-two times mentioned in Matthew and no where else.

I advise you to go read them all and try to understand their signification. Jesus said it was like a fish that was cleaned of its guts. When this is translated in English it means a person who repented from all its sins. See Matthew 13, 48.

When the bad, the devil, the sin are out of us by a sincere repentance; we enter the kingdom of heaven and we can stay in it until we sin again. I feel so great in it and because I love my God with all of my heart, my soul and my thoughts, I don't ever want to get out of it. Now, Jesus said that the church leaders of his time were shutting off the kingdom of heaven from people or in people faces. See Matthew 23, 13. 'But woe to you, scribes and Pharisees, hypocrites, (priests, bishops, archbishops, cardinals, popes and pastors and all of Paul's products) because you shut off the kingdom of heaven from people, for you don't enter it yourselves, nor do you allow those who are entering to go in.'

Now, if the Paul's disciples and all these leaders can shut off the kingdom of heaven from people with their lies and their brainwashing and their contradictions; this means that the Jesus' disciples can open it with the truth, with the true word of God. This is what Jesus did when he gave to Peter the keys of the kingdom of heaven and it is most likely the reason why Paul attacked him so violently. See Matthew 16, 19. 'I will give you the keys of the kingdom of heaven, and whatever you bind on earth shall be bound in heaven and whatever you loose on earth shall be loosed in heaven.'

So, everyone should be careful of how they treat the Jesus' disciples.

The church lied when it said Peter was the first bishop of Rome. Peter was brought in Rome as a prisoner and killed by the Romans too, but he was never a bishop. He was way too faithful to Jesus to disobey even at the cost of his life. Peter died murdered in Rome, in a deadly town where the Jesus' disciples weren't welcomed at all. I strongly believe it would be extremely dangerous for me to go over there to speak about what I know. It would more or less be suicidal. It would be dangerous anywhere, but even more over there. It would be also extremely dangerous for me to go speak about the things I know; even a little of it in any Christian church either it is Catholic or Protestant.

It is even dangerous to speak about this to anyone and I say to everyone to be very careful in the assemblies of the Bible's studies; especially if you're not with Jesus' disciples. I believe these studies are made to detect the ones who follow Jesus instead of Paul. I quickly found out that my ideas, my thoughts and my knowledge on the word of God were not welcomed in these pagan churches. Could you just imaging Louis Riel going to Rome and tell the pope that the rest of the world should separate from it? He said it in court, in Saskatchewan and they killed him.

Only an apostle like Paul could live in peace in Rome and he is the first bishop of this town, the first of his category. Peter was told to go after the lost sheep of the house of Israel and I'm sure he listened to Jesus until his death. See Matthew 10, 5-6. 'These twelve (including Peter) Jesus sent out after instructing them: "Do not go in the way of the Gentiles (like Romans) and do not enter the towns of the Samaritans; but rather go to the lost sheep of the house of Israel." '

I am persuaded that Peter was faithful to Jesus to his death, faithful to his Master; no matter what the liars tried to make us believe. The reasons the church said Peter was the Rome first bishop is to take the suspicion off Paul and to give to itself some credits as a Christian church.

See in Acts 28, 30-31 what Paul did. 'And Paul stayed two full years in his own rented quarters and was welcoming all who came to him, preaching the <u>kingdom of God</u> and teaching the Lord Jesus Christ with all openness, unhindered.'

Jesus preached the kingdom of heaven, not the kingdom of God and they are different from one another.

The only way this could be done in Rome at the time of Paul was because Paul preached against the word of the true God, against the teaching of Jesus just like they are still doing. It was totally forbidden to talk about the true God in those days in Rome and Jesus' friends and disciples were Cesar's enemies. According to Acts 18, 2, no Jew could stay in Rome. 'Because Claudius had commanded all the Jews to leave Rome!'

This was also at the time of Paul in Rome.

According to John 19, 12, no one could be friend to Jesus and to Caesar. 'If you release this man, you are no friend of Caesar; everyone who makes himself out to be a king opposes Caesar.'

Everyone who spoke about the true God or in favour of the true God and in favour of Jesus of Nazareth also opposed Caesar.

Paul couldn't be friend of Jesus and of Caesar and to be able to live in peace in Rome he had to be with Caesar and against Jesus, simple as this.

Jesus said that the least in the kingdom of heaven was greater than John the Baptist. I only have one explanation about this declaration and this is John the Baptist ran out of faith. After all he has seen and heard about Jesus, besides being Jesus' cousin; John the Baptist sent his disciples asking Jesus if he should expect another Messiah. See Matthew 11, 3. 'Are you the expected one or should we look for someone else?'

Jesus must have felt like crying when he heard this.

In Matthew and according to the prophets before Jesus; when Jesus was questioned before his death he wouldn't have opened his mouth and this is for his defence. See Isaiah 53, 7. 'He was oppressed and he was afflicted, yet he did not open his mouth: Like a lamb that is led to slaughter and like a sheep that is silent before its shearers, so he did not open his mouth.'

To be like a lamb is not being a lamb and being like a sheep is not being a sheep, an animal like God's enemies said he was and they still say he is. This is an abomination in the holy place, in the Holy Bible like Jesus talked about in Matthew 24, 15. Just like coming like a thief is not being a thief.

Now go read Matthew 27, 11-14 and you will see that Jesus didn't open his mouth, for his defence that is. After this go read Jesus in his interrogation in John 18, 12 to 19, 16 and you will see it is not the same Jesus at all and the one in John fought back just like Paul did it at his trial. We can say for sure the one in the gospel of John didn't keep his mouth shut. Read Acts 23.

There is another thing we find in John 20 which is quite questionable. We were told Jesus rose from the dead in the morning of the first day of the week.

We were also told Jesus died on Friday afternoon around three. Jesus said himself, see Matthew 12, 40. 'For just as Jonah was <u>three days and three nights</u> in the belly of a sea monster, so will <u>the Son of Man be three days and three nights in the heart of the earth</u>.'

Now, according to the word of God; either Jesus died on Thursday afternoon and rose on Sunday afternoon or he died on Friday afternoon and rose on the second day of the week, but from Friday afternoon to Sunday morning; this only makes two nights and not quite two full days. We don't really need to be a scientist or a university student to count up to three, do we?

Why I never heard anyone talking about this one is beyond me. Do we trust our church leaders so blindly? Maybe they said this is a mystery like they often did. This is very possible because the main goal of the devil is to deceive the world just like he did in the Garden of Eden.

According to Jonah 2, 1, Jonah was really three days and three nights in the belly of a big fish.

As for the end of time Jesus said that even him and neither the angels knew when it will come; that only God the Father does. But Jesus gave us a lot of clues about it. See Matthew 24 from verse 37 to 42. 'For the coming of the Son of Man will be just like the days of Noah. For in those days before the flood they were eating and drinking, marrying and giving in marriage until Noah entered the ark and they did not understand until the flood came and took them all away; so will the coming of the Son of Man be. Then there will be two men in the field, one will be taken and one will be left.

Two women will be grinding at the mill, one will be taken and one will be left. Therefore be on the alert, for you don't know which day your Lord is coming.'

There are two important things to consider in those last verses. The first one is that one person out of two will be taken. The day that the Lord God will have nothing more to gain by leaving the weeds with the wheat, the lies with the truth, the liar with the righteous is the day He will hit with his anger the impious of this world.

At this point and time we have to believe that the bad didn't overpower the good just yet. It was said that the powers of heaven will be shaken. Matthew 24, 29. 'But immediately after the tribulation of those days the sun will be darkened and the moon will not give its light and the stars will fall from the sky and the powers of heaven will be shaken.'

I'm pretty sure this is happening with all of the trips they are taking in the space.

The second thing Jesus said is they were all taken away. Who were taken away in the time of Noah? The answer is very simple; they were the impious, the sinners. The same thing will happen in the coming of the Son of Man. The Son of Man said it, not me. Then the Paul who said he will be taken away with all of his followers admitted by his own declarations that he is not on Jesus side. See 1 Thessalonians 4, 17.

It is true that he will be taken, but I can't help sympathizing with all the people who let themselves being put to sleep or blinded by this miserable liar.

I only hope that my book will be read soon enough to open the eyes of the biggest number. One thing I know for sure and this is it is by the will of God I'm writing all those things and it is not for me, because God has already opened my eyes, but

He needs to open the yes of many more and there are not these many ways to do just that.

If I take example on Louis Riel's life; it is a lot better for me to write instead of talking. It is a lot more being shrewd like snakes and this will allow me to alert a lot more people.

Another thing to remember about what Jesus said on his return and what happened at the time of Noah is the fact the impious didn't know the flood was coming; that they were going to lose their life, but Noah and his family knew it. And even if Noah was telling the impious about it; they were laughing and mocking him until the waters took them all away.

All the people who will laugh at my books, at my warnings and about what I say can expect the same ending. No one can mock God, his word and his warnings forever unpunished; this is a sure thing. See Deuteronomy 18, 19. 'It shall come about that whoever will not listen to my words which Jesus shall speak in my name, I Myself will require it of him.'

I just understood at this moment why none of my books got published yet. In fact one did, my first one, but the publisher went brook and the book got no where. The day my books will be on the market my life wouldn't be worth a penny. I will have to hide and there are not this many places I can do this safely. Even in Israel, the city of the Great King, I will be in danger. Just like Jesus was I won't be able to find a place to rest my head or to write in peace. The least you can say is I take the warnings of Jesus seriously.

Last year on the news I heard that three atheists wrote books on atheism and each one of them sold more than ten millions copies without been bothered by Rome or anyone. Do you see? It's because them too are with the devil. We cannot serve two masters.

Practically every religious people on earth will be a threat to me, because they think protecting an institution crated by Jesus when in fact it was created by Paul, the devil, the Jesus and God's enemy who created the Christians churches and many others. The worst is that no one, not even my own sisters take the time to go check the truth even after they were informed.

All these people who say the Bible is the absolute truth! The truth that the truth and the lies are there together in the Bible is there too.

See Matthew 13, 26. 'But when the wheat sprouted and bore grain, then the tares became evident also.'

Jesus sowed the truth, but the lies showed up too, and no matter how hard I looked; none other than Paul and his children came to sow the lies in the Bible and contradict Jesus, the apostles and God. Besides, Jesus who sowed the truth said his enemy who sowed the lies was the devil. See Matthew 13, 39. 'And the enemy who sowed them is the devil.'

Louis Riel understood all of this, but he unfortunately tried to save some of Paul disciples, the demons, the priests, the bishops and some archbishops whom had only one goal in life and this was to prolong the lies to the end, but their end is here or else their end is getting close. The only fact I understood these things will probably allow me to live a bit longer.

Just before my first marriage at the age of twenty-four I had a long conversation with a priest who was to marry us. I had understood a lot of things by then without realizing I was talking to one of Jesus' enemy. I pointed out to him that the church was doing a lot of things contrary to the teaching of Jesus. I have to say here that I met him at the request of my wife to be; who was a bit scared of my knowledge of the Bible that was opposite to what she knew. I succeeded to get her out of the Catholic Church, but I cannot get her out of the Baptist Evangelist Church.

To this priest I spoke about the baptism they do to the babies even before they have their eyes opened or believe in what so ever. I talked about the confession, them who confess people when it is written in Jeremiah 17, 5. 'Thus says the Lord; 'Cursed is the man who trusts in mankind and make flesh his strength and whose heart turns away from the Lord.' '

When Jesus talked about confession he had a total different signification. See Matthew 10, 32. 'Therefore everyone who confesses me before men, I will also confess him before my Father who is in heaven.'

The meaning of confess here is testify. If I translate this in my own words it goes like this: 'This is why anyone who testify of the exact and real truth I taught my disciples, I will in turn testify for him before my Father in heaven.

I talked to this priest about the second God's commandment (Exodus 20, 4) that says not to make any images of what is in heaven above or on the earth beneath or in the water under the earth and their churches are full of statues, crucifix, (the way of the cross). I also talked about the fact he let people call him father; something Jesus has completely forbidden to his disciples to do.

His only response was to tell me the church was young. I retorted telling him I was only in my early twenties; that I had not much education and I could understand those things. All he said to my future wife of the time is that my faith was developed more than the average people. He made me only one recommendation and this was that I absolutely had to join a religion, no matter which one, but I had to join one for my salvation.

Do you see? He knew very well that if I join one religion I would still be a slave of the devil, no matter which denomination I join and the sooner the better for him, because this way I will be no longer a threat to his congregation. This priest was the leader of the Bible's studies and me; I had only a grade six education back then. It was much later that I resumed my high school.

When it comes to baptize the babies before they open their eyes is nothing less than make them slaves, proselytes even before they can choose their own destiny. They do it on the pretence to save them from the guilt, the sin of our first parents (Adam and Eve) when we cannot be responsible for the sins of our parents. If you doubt what I'm saying go read Ezekiel 18 completely and you will see that the children are not responsible for the sins of their parents and the parents are not responsible for the sins of their children which make senses anyway. Then look at Matthew 5, 17 to see what Jesus said about the prophets who were there before him and this includes Ezekiel. 'Do not think that I came to abolish the law or <u>the prophets</u>; I did not come to abolish them but to fulfill.'

You have read right; Jesus said that he didn't come to abolish the law, on the other hand his enemy, Paul said just the contrary by saying that Jesus abolished the law by dying on the cross. Read very carefully Ephesians 2, 15. 'By abolishing in his flesh the enmity, which is the law of commandments contained in ordinances, so that in himself he might make the two into one new man, thus establish peace.'

Now look what Jesus said about establishing peace. Read Matthew 10, 34. 'Do not think that I came to bring peace on earth; I did not come to bring peace, but a sword.'

CHAPTER 4

When we read in the New Testament, which is over ninety per cent from Paul; you will see that he hates the law, that he abolished it or tried to, that he said it is old and gone, that we're no longer under the law, but that we are under the grace. See Romans 6, 14. 'For sin shall not be master over you, for you are not under the law but under grace.'

Sin has no power over those who don't believe in God either, but this wouldn't spare them from the judgement of God; either they believe in Him or not. The fact remains that God exists and He holds each one of us responsible for our actions; especially if we didn't repent.

Paul said we are no longer under the law of God, that they are under grace and that sin has no power over them and yet; they say they all have sin. What kind of grace is this?

All the benedictions are coming from God and they come to us because we obey the laws, the ordinances and his statutes. You can find the confirmation about this in Genesis 26, 4-5.

Either I believe in the laws of men or not; if I kill someone there is a good chance that I will be punished by those laws.

I could talk about this subject for a long time, because Paul spent a lot of time to convince people that the laws of God are gone and they were replaced by the grace. Jesus said that we couldn't follow two masters. See Matthew 6, 24.

I say to you that you cannot follow Jesus and follow Paul. Either you're listening to Jesus and stay under the law of God or else you're listening to Paul, the liar, the murderer, the blasphemer, the deceiver and then you will be lost with him. You cannot be at the same time with Jesus, the one who tells the truth and at the same time be with Paul, the one who lies, because they don't stand together. According to 2 Thessalonians 2, 10 we have to receive the love for the truth to be saved. We still need to know what the truth is. There is where I come in, to continue the work of Jesus, the work of the Jesus' disciples, to preach the repentance like Jesus did and he asked us to do; to heal the sick and resurrect the dead like he did.

It's the sick who needs the doctor, the sinners who need the word of God, the truth. See Matthew 9, 12.

There are times when all this seems to be useless; it is a bit like to try to save someone from drowning. This same person could bring you under without worrying a bit about your well-being, but we do it anyway and we ignore the risk, the danger being careful and doing for the best. I saved a childhood friend one time from drowning when I was young, but I had the wisdom to grab him from behind where he had no possibility to hurt me. One thing I noticed at that time is the fact he was completely lost. He didn't even know where he was and it took quite a few minutes before he realized what happened. There was only water up to his shoulders, but in his panic he didn't realize it.

I am aware though that I am very helpless before the huge mission which is awaiting me. I know too the power is in the word of God and God is the Almighty. I do the work I have to do and I know God will do what He has to do when the time comes.

Although, I have the annoying habit to want to save certain people myself and I have to remember what Jesus himself said in Matthew 6, 10, 7, 21, 10, 24, 12, 50, 18, 14 and 26, 42. And this is; 'Your will be done on earth as it is in heaven.'

I just hope it will be my will too. I might just want to save someone who doesn't want to be saved or else someone God doesn't want. Abraham did it when he wanted to save Sodom and Gomorrah. See Genesis 18, 31. 'Abraham said; 'Now behold,

I have ventured to speak to the Lord; suppose twenty (righteous) are found there?' And God said; 'I will not destroy it on account of the twenty.' '

I too says; not mine Lord, but may your will be done and everything will be fine. I only want to do like Jesus and Louis Riel; meaning to do everything You will command me Lord. Here is another song of mine that I like particularly.

It's Good Oh Lord

It's good to recognize your voice oh Lord
It's good to know about your laws
It's good to have You as a King oh Lord
It's good to have You as a shield.
Keep me always by your sight
I always want to be with You.
No where there's anyone as bright
Spare me from your anger too.
2
It's good to experience your peace, oh Lord
It's good to know that I love You.
It's good to know that I know You, oh Lord
It's good, You are the goodness too.
You delivered me from evil
When I did receive your word.
I'm not scared of the devil
You showed me how to use the sword. (The word of God)
3
You showed me much of your mercy, oh Lord
By chasing away the demons.
By You I was invited oh Lord
Blessed the one who sees your forms
They will always be happy
For listening to Jesus
All those who carried their cross

The ones that You have chosen
4
You showed me some of your powers, oh Lord
By Jesus, Moses and the prophets
It's You who are the deliverance, oh Lord
I respect your Sabbaths and your will
It's good to recognize your voice
It's good to know about your laws.
It's good to have You as a King.
It's good to have You as a shield.

All the abominations that I found in the Bible inspired me
another song called:

See The Abomination.

Abomination cause of desolation. Matthew 24, 15.
Is well established in the temple of God
The imagination of this damnation
Is there and forces its way to the Kingdom.
Matthew 11, 12
The violent men take it by force
With their lies they take you away from God
They have for support the lies that destroy
An angel told me one night in my dream.
2
Where is the temple? Know that it is within us
It's Him who made us to his likeness.
Made us with nothing and Jesus the humble
Said that He shares his home and garden.
Won't you believe what God said to us?
Won't you open your ears and hear his words?
Won't you see why Jesus suffered so much?
Won't you let your spirit receive his messages?

Of course it makes me sad to see all the ones I love refusing even to go look for the abominable things I pointed out to them from the Bible, but there is no way I can force them to do so. I am pretty sure too that if they do; they would see what I saw and they would join me in my journey, who knows? Some of them might also join the ones who would want my death or yet just say that I became crazy like Louis Riel.

Jesus too was saddened by the fact his people refused to receive him, to receive the truth. See Matthew 23, 37. 'Jerusalem, Jerusalem, who kills the prophets and stones those who are sent to her! How often I wanted to gather your children together, the way a hen gathers her chicks under her wings and you were unwilling.'

But just like Jesus I understood the weeping and the gnashing of teeth were not for the children of God. This doesn't mean we're not sad for the ones who didn't see the kingdom of heaven yet. If only I was sure to have a few students I wouldn't hesitate a single minute to open a school for these blinds; so I could open their eyes like Jesus was doing and still do for the ones who believe in him enough to listen to him.

Politics and religions

In my opinion the politic and the religion are connected one way or the other, because wars are created by one or by the other or by both. Take the revolutions of the Métis of the years 1870 and 1885 were created by the injustices from the government of the John A. Macdonald and the response of this same Canadian government against a group of people who didn't want to be Catholics or Christians anymore.

Of course because they didn't have the protection from the priests, the bishops and the archbishops of their time anymore; this government chose to crush this people instead of making their life easier with some reasonable accommodations like some farms properly surveyed and something to put on the table.

We don't need to have a university degree to understand their demands were more than reasonable and the real reasons to crush Riel and his people were other than financial. As far as I can tell it would have been a lot cheaper to help this people than to fight it, but it was very important for the government and for the religions to shut up this movement of truth, the word of God that was going to revolutionize the world; especially if this was going to be done by a half breed, a Métis. A half breed, a half Indian who was going to show the truth, morality to the clergy and to the government. This was absolutely out of the question; they couldn't afford this.

Although Louis Riel has to be a happy man, because Jesus said it. See Matthew 5, 10-12. 'Blessed are those who have been persecuted for the sake of righteousness, for theirs is the kingdom of heaven. Blessed are you when people insult you and persecute you, and falsely say all kind of evil against you because of me. (the word of God) Rejoice and be glad, for your reward in heaven is great; for in the same way they persecuted the prophets who were before you.'

I made a song to honour Louis Riel and to ask justice for him and his people, but I never made any for John A.

Macdonald. I didn't make any for Paul or for the Christians churches except for the church of Jesus.

He Was Only A Man

He was nothing, but he was fair, was nobody.
Who did something for his people, he was a man.
Was elected, was evicted fought all the way.
His victory, our history, the guy has won.
A patriot, strong will fighter, a Canadian.
Gave his best shot as a worker until the end.
Recognition from the nation is essential.
Cause with his life, he paid the price, this was Riel.
Course
Riel, you're a hero, now lot of people know.
That you were innocent for the crime you were sent.
Riel, you're a hero, now lot of people know.
You didn't deserve to die this way under the sky.
Riel, you're a hero, now lot of people know.
That your cause is not lost; it's heard and it's a must.
Riel, you're the hero, now lot of people know.
I told many of them, your home is the Heavens. Matthew 5, 10.
2
And he had faith, this Canadian until the end.
In his country who betrayed him and all his friends.
Will he get paid for all the aid he contributed?
For the rights of Métis and whites, Native's disputes.
His sacrificed most of his life for the settlers.
It would be nice, to see his rights for the others.
It's not in vain, he fought the shame, it's our glory.
His cause today democracy, our victory!
Course
Riel, you're a hero, now lot of people know.
That you were innocent for the crime you were sent.
Riel, you're a hero, now lot of people know.

You didn't deserve to die this way under the sky.
Riel, you're a hero, now lot of people know.
That your cause is not lost; it's heard and it's a must.
Riel, you're the hero, now lot of people know.
I told many of them, your home is the Heavens.
I told many of them, your home is the Heavens.
Matthew 5, 10.

Jesus was hanged to the post and so did Louis Riel, but according to Paul; they both are cursed, damned because of it and Paul is saying at the same time that the Law of God is a malediction. See Galatians 3, 13. 'Christ redeemed us from the <u>curse</u> of the Law, having become a curse for us, for it is written, 'Cursed is everyone who hangs on a tree.' '

What is beyond me is, how could the people who is responsible of what is going in the Bible and what is not have left such an abomination in there?

It is kind of curious, but I made some searches to find another place where this could have been written in the Bible, but it could not be found any where else than in Galatians 3, 13, in Paul's book.

To say that to love God with all of our heart, with all of our soul and with all of our thoughts is a curse is to say one of the worst abominations there is and I think only the devil is capable of this and Paul could. You can make up your own mind about it; it is up to you.

Louis Riel must be reinstated in the Canadian history in the same degree than the Des-Ormeaux, the Laviolette, Champlain, Jacques Cartier and many others if not as a politician; let it be as a persecuted prophet, a martyr. We talked about a lot of other martyrs who didn't do as much for their people or for their country and for God.

It's not his country and neither his people Louis Riel betrayed, but the Catholic Church he wanted to pull away from and to denounce with some good reasons too. They should have given him a medal of honour for his courage and for what he has done. What ever; like I said before; his reward is in the kingdom of heaven. For what I say about it in this world it's more for people who want to give him what ever belongs to him by rights and for the justice; him who fought for men's rights.

The Catholic Church cost the country a lot more money than Louis Riel so far and it's not over just yet with all the lawsuits that come forward against its members every so often. If Louis Riel was interested in little boys like many priests are; he would surely have stayed with the clergy.

I made a joke years ago and I told it to one of my friends, but the problem was that I told it to her in front of her kids who were watching TV and didn't seem to pay attention to what we were saying. The question was; what is the priest's penis use for other than to pee? The young boy who heard it went to ask his school teacher who was a nun and when he told us about it; he couldn't stop laughing. It was more of a riddle than a joke. Of course we were both anxious to find out what was the nun response, but he said she wanted to know the answer which is; ça sert d'os. Translated in English it gives you; use as a bone. To understand it you need to know that priesthood in French is sacerdoce. When we asked the boy what the nun said he told us that she said this was a good one.

It's good to laugh a little in life and apparently it's very good for your heath. Some people I'm sure will condemn me for this one, but those priests have abused and scandalized enough children to deserve this little laugh. Not only they did a lot of wrong doing, but they were also protected by their superiors; which is in my opinion a worst crime yet. I don't condemn them, but just like Jesus did; I ask how could they avoid the judgement and the punishment of hell? Only the sincere repentance could be the answer and believe me; God knows the heart and the thoughts of everyone of us. Not me but Jesus said they wouldn't enter the kingdom of heaven. See Matthew 23, 13. 'But woe to you scribes and Pharisees, hypocrites, (priests, bishops and archbishops and all this bunch) because you shut off the kingdom of heaven from people; for you don't enter in yourselves, nor you let the ones who want to enter, entering.'

Like Jesus said it; the prostitutes and the tax collectors will enter it before them.

It is very difficult to know how much Louis Riel knew about the word of God, because of the screening that was done on his writings. One thing is sure; I will do everything I can to spread my writings in many different places and with many different people so the beast, no matter how dangerous it is will have a hard time to destroy everything. The beast will have to kill many people before it could eliminate all of what God gave me. One thing is sure and this is the beast will do everything it can to choke the truth again. To tell you the truth; I don't know anyone at this time on whom I can totally trust to entrust all I got and how could I know who is going to betray me. I don't have the power or the knowledge to know the future, but yet maybe God will warn me on time and will guide me through this. Jesus had one trader out of twelve and I expect to have maybe one faithful out of twelve. I reassure myself thinking about Louis Riel who had many faithful friends like Gabriel Dumont, his secretary Will Jackson and many more, I'm sure. In fact I was already betrayed by members of my own family and friends who know some of the information and went to talk to their pastors about it.

One thing is written for quite some time now is the ones who don't have the mark of the beast will have to hide, to flee and they will be persecuted across the world, but I rather suffer for a short time this is than to suffer for the eternity, because no suffering could measure up with hell. If there is one prayer I wouldn't mind to repeat it would be to ask God for the strength to stay strong until the end; no matter how bad is the threat I'm facing.

Many people thought Peter was a coward for disowning Jesus three times. I would like to see those people or rather see their reaction before certain death or torture. Peter is the one who had the most faith, the most courage and the most repentance. There is a very good reason why Jesus gave him the keys of the kingdom of heaven. There was a very good reason too why God dispersed all the apostles that day. If God didn't disperse them we would have nothing or not much from the teaching of Jesus today. Not only Jesus would have wasted three years of his life; he would have also died in vain, for nothing, because all of his apostles would have died crucified with him and it would have been no testimony left.

Rome did everything it could back then too to eliminate the truth and people who were spreading it. Rome even tried to eliminate Jesus right from his birth and proved to the world it was antichrist and anti God. The history is all there written for you and Rome cannot deny the murders of many baby boys of less than two years old around Bethlehem.

Despite of so many efforts and despite of so many murders like the murders of Jesus and Louis Riel and all of the Jesus' disciples since Jesus began to teach; Rome didn't succeed to eliminate the truth completely. See Matthew 16, 18. 'I also say to you that you are Peter and upon this rock I will build my church and the gates of Hades will not overpower it.'

The church of Jesus is the truth, the word of God and this is why the gates of Hades will not overpower it.

It is not because it didn't try though, with all of its inquisitions, its crusades and its wars. Rome did a lot of harm and I really think it will do just this until it's completely destroyed. The devil is way too proud to repent and the head of the beast too.

Where would its friends go after its destruction? This is for me a bubble gum mystery. Maybe some of them will see the light and walk towards it, but the most would want to follow their idols all the way to hell where their friends are. Despite everything the beast did, I mean its crimes and its threats; here I am writing about the truth and I got enough to make it very furious.

These days they are talking a lot about the residential schools; especially the ones in the West Canadian of the years

1870 until 1996. They especially talk about the abuses done to the Métis and to the Natives' children of Manitoba and Saskatchewan. It crossed my mind it could very well be because of the messages left by Louis Riel to his people. Why were these children forced to these schools if not for some very serious reasons and very critical like the survival of the Catholic Church and Christianity in general.

No one can really say without a laugh they did it because they care about the natives and about the Métis; especially coming from the Prime Minister of the time, John A. Macdonald who proved his hatred for them and backed by the clergymen of his time. It's obvious that the members of the clergy as always didn't care about Natives except maybe for their own personal sexual interests and others.

I strongly believe though that some more important reasons pushed them to take charge of the Natives and the Métis' children and one of them would have been to find out who knew some of the truth Louis Riel sowed before his death. The same principle applied by Paul has to be respected by his followers; they had to shut them up at all cost.

This would explain why such a big number of children never returned home alive and some of them were never heard of anymore. It's only a hypothesis, but it seems to me obvious. I believe it, because God doesn't give me useless visions.

I went to read on the Web about the residential schools in English; the West ones and they are closed since 1996 because of their bad reputation when in French; in the East on the contrary they are overwhelmed with praises. This is kind of strange, isn't it?

On the news these days they're talking a lot about the air India plane accident too; saying it's the biggest murderous disaster of Canadian history. I really think this is totally wrong. The Christian religions have killed a lot more people than this plane crash, but one thing is very similar in both scandals; this is the responsible people of those crimes were never punished. In the same way the responsible people of the crash were never punished; the responsible people of the torture and murders of these children at the residential schools were never punished either.

When I heard on the news that some of the government and some of the clergy representatives were present at this gigantic inquiry commission for the healing and pardon for what happened; I got shivers in my back. If Murray Sinclair who is the chief commissioner of this important inquiry is really sincere in finding what really happened, the truth, he has to get rid of the representatives who have some big interests in keeping the lid on this shitty cooking pot for them.

They're talking about the victims of the residential schools of the West as survivors, but we cannot forget to talk about the ones who didn't survive of the crimes from the hands of these murderers. They were not only victims but they were also martyrs for knowing a bit of the truth. This last phrase is for the ones who think I am a bit crazy for saying that my life is at risk for telling the truth. This beast is powerful, but just wait; up until now it was only on the defensive side; pretty soon it will be on the attack. Read Matthew 24, 22. 'Unless those days had been cut short, no life would have been saved; but for the sake of the elect, those days will be cut short.'

What happened in the residential schools was on a small scale; the time of a much larger scale, a world wide scale is near. I don't want to diminish at all what happened; the crimes of the beast are real bad, but the worst is yet to come. Worst than we ever had Jesus told us. See Matthew 24, 21. 'For then there will be a great tribulation, such as has not occurred since the beginning of the world until now, nor ever will.'

This seems to be real bad for the children of God, but it's nothing at all compared to what are awaiting the children of the devil and his angels. Here is how I see this; it will be a short tribulation for the children of God, but an eternal hell for the children of the devil. Now the choice is yours though, because when the good news of the kingdom of heaven is spread out; the one I'm sending out through the entire world to serve as a testimony will be known. then the end will come. There will be no turning back. It is written in Matthew 24, 14. 'This gospel of the kingdom of heaven shall be preached in the whole world as a testimony to all the nations, and then the end will come.'

For sure there will be some resistance from the beast, but with the speed of the Internet nowadays; news travel at the speed of the light and it won't take this long for this news to go around the world; just like the news of the pastor Jones who wants to burn the Qur'an on the eleven of September. Two days after his declaration the whole world knew about it. It was a controversial one and those travel even faster than all the other news.

Jesus was killed because the beast wanted to shut up the truth, Louis Riel was killed to shut up the truth, one and a half million Jews were killed in the years 67 to 73 to shut up the truth that Jesus had spread out, some of the children of the residential schools of the West were tortured and killed to shut up the truth that Louis Riel had spread out, many others were killed for the same reasons and if Murray Sinclair finds out the truth, take my word for it; they will shut him up too.

Nothing is more important for the beast than to keep a lid on this shit, those sordid crimes, but one day will come where it won't be able to do it anymore and it will be then this beast will break loose until the day it will be chained for a thousand years. Only then it will be wonderful for the children of God to live on this earth.

In Revelation 11, 10 it is written in there that two prophets have tormented the inhabitants of the earth and the reason for them to be tormented is very simple; these inhabitants just found out they were living with the lies and they served the liar, the creator of the religions, Paul instead of listening to Jesus, the one who is telling the truth, the one who wanted to set them free from these same religions, free from this slavery, free from evil.

Up until now I don't really know whom to talk to that wouldn't be any risk for my life, because religions are antichrist, the governments are antichrist, the police and the army are also sworn in, which is antichrist too according to Jesus, the Christ.

See in Matthew 5, 34-37 and if you read these three verses carefully you'll find out that what ever is above your word is coming from the devil and none and nothing is more antichrists than the devil.

At the time of the ancient kings a king always had a wise man, an adviser, a prophet or else a seer to advise him and woe to the one who was wrong; jail and even death was for him. If I was our Prime Minister, Stephen Harper adviser; I would certainly tell him that abortion doesn't please God and neither the gay marriages. I would tell him too that the swearing practice in their ceremonies, in our court of justice and the swearing of our police and army officers are totally antichrist. I would surely tell him too that to receive God's benedictions we have to be on his side first. I don't see why not a solemn promise could just do the same thing. I don't think it is very necessary to involve God in our corrupted businesses. Paul did it, but he also proved he wasn't on God's side. But our Prime minister most likely knows all this, but his choices are limited.

Could we only imaging if anytime the pope, the bishops, the archbishops, the cardinals, the priests and the pastors would stand up to say we have to put the Canadian Government down because it is antichrist? What would happen if they say we have to take arms if necessary? Everyone to whom their religion is their god wouldn't hesitate very long to follow their idols.

They didn't hesitate either to take the children who had the possibility to know some messages of Jesus that Louis Riel could have spread out. It must had worked, because even if I spent most of my life reading in the Bible; I had to have a dream from God at the age of forty-eight to open my eyes on this reality that we were dominated by the beast.

God has his own way to come to get us, but still we have to recognize it. Thanks to Jesus, thanks to Louis Riel and thanks to God.

I hope you like the songs I made from my God, because I got many of them. I think this one is an eye opener as well and is to me very special and it's called:

The Jesus' Messages

'Just remember long time ago in my journey into this world. Matthew 4, 17.

I told you everything I know about my Father's Holy Word.

That I didn't come to abolish neither the law or the prophets. Matthew 5, 17.

And until all is accomplished, everything stands don't you forget. Matthew 5, 18.

I said not the smallest letter and not the least stroke of a pen. Matthew 5, 18.

None from the law of my Father will disappear so understand.. Matthew 5, 19.

But what did tell you the liar? That with my flesh onto the cross. Gen. 3, 1 and Ephesians 2, 16.

I destroyed law and barrier, rules and commandments for the lost. Ephesians 2, 14.

One asked me what was the greatest of the commandments in the law. Matthew 22, 35-36

It was just to put me to test;

He tried to find in me a flaw.

Love your God with all of your heart, with all your soul and all your mind. Matthew 22, 37.

From your neighbour don't be apart Mat, 22, 39. Follow those two and you'll be mine. Mat, 22, 40.

But what did tell you the liar? That the whole law is one command. Galatians 5, 14.

And this is to love your neighbour as yourself, see now where he stands.

Doesn't speak about my Father, cause sinners too love who loves them. Matthew 5, 46.

It's good to love one another, but that won't get you to heaven.

Who's my mother? Who's my brother? Who are my sisters and my friends? Matthew 12, 48-50.
He does the will of my Father; my Father who is in heaven. Matthew 6, 9.
You are the salt of all the earth. You are the light cause you believe. Matthew 5, 13-14.
Even though sometime you get hurt, watch out for the one who deceives. Matthew 16, 24- 24, 4.
I sent you like sheep in the field through wolves so be careful for your sake. Matthew 10, 16.
And like doves have God for your shield, so therefore be shrewd as snakes.
He is clever the enemy in manipulating the truth. Genesis 3, 1, 2 Corinthians 12, 16.
He is more crafty than any; see he made Eve pick up the fruit.
So you will have for enemy for sure members of your own house. Matthew 10, 37.
You will not be worthy of me; not if you love more someone else.
To the earth then I brought the sword; so take your cross and follow me. Matthew 10, 34, 16, 24.
You won't be worthy of the Lord if you put first your family. Matthew 10, 37.
I'm the one who sowed the good seed; they are the sons of the kingdom. Matthew 13, 37-38.
My enemy who sowed the weeds and they all are the devil's sons. Matthew 13, 38-39.
One day I will send my angels to through the weeds in the furnace. Matthew 13, 41-42.
There will be then no more rebels, you'll shine like the sun in this place. Matthew 13, 41 and 43.
Just remember long time ago in my journey into this world. Matthew 4, 17.

I told you everything I know about my Father's
Holy Word.
That I didn't come to abolish neither the law or
the prophets. Matthew 5, 17.
And until all is accomplished, everything stands
don't you forget. Matthew 5, 18.
Everything stands don't you forget.'

As you can verify it for yourselves; this last song is entirely
from Jesus' messages only.

Jesus, the true prophet, <u>the Son of Man</u> told us himself who
he was. Look in Matthew 9, 8 to see what is written. 'But when
the crowd saw this, they were awestruck and glorified God, who
had given such authority to <u>men</u>.

God gave to men like Jesus, Moses, Joseph and Riel the
power to open people eyes even if those are solidly closed. I
know one thing and this is God gave me, I think enough
information to put in this book to open the eyes of the entire
world. I only hope it will be translate in every possible language.
See Matthew 28, 19-20. 'Go therefore and make disciples of all
nations, teaching them <u>to observe all that I commanded you</u>;
and lo, I am with you always, even to the end of the age.'

And yes, the word of God is still here with us and it will be
here up to the end.

You will tell me that I didn't write; baptizing them in the
name of the Father and the son and the Holy Spirit. The reason
is simple; it's because Jesus never said this. He never baptized
anyone himself, at least not with water. He baptized his disciples
with the truth, with all the teaching that came from God the
Father, like not to judge, not to swear, not to worry, to be on the
alert, to pray, whom to pray and a thousand other things and I'm
pretty sure the beast has cut off a bunch of them; especially some
messages that could hurt the teaching of the Christian churches.
Water and fire don't mix very well.

Jesus would have never talked to his disciples or to his apostles about baptism until his last day on earth which I find very questionable, very strange. I think the last part of Matthew 28, 19 was added to the gospel and this wasn't done by Matthew at all. When Jesus gave his instructions to his twelve apostles he didn't mention the baptism at all. See Matthew 10, 1-42.

I still wonder how come there are enough messages left in the Bible to allow me to discover and to identify the beast. Maybe it's a trap set up to catch disciples like me who have the courage to tell the truth even at the cost of their lives. I found some places in the Bible where the writing was modified, some things that didn't sound right to some people who went to talk to their pastors about it. I have chosen the washing of the feet that you can find in John's gospel only. To show you what I mean by this and it doesn't make sense at all probably because this wasn't the John of Jesus. The story is written in John 13, 4. 'Jesus got up from supper and laid aside <u>his garments</u>; and taking a towel he covered his parts with it. Then he poured water into the basin and began to wash his disciples' feet and to wipe them with the towel which he was girded.'

This guy, this John liked the nakedness of men and we will see it again a bit further. In the newer Bibles Jesus takes off his outer garment instead of his garments, but when he put his clothes back on again, it's written his garments, which it's written in John 13, 12. Now they changed parts of the story because it doesn't make sense that the son of God; whom they say is God would have got completely naked in front of his disciples????????

It would make more senses today, but in those days men didn't even undress to make babies and it was still like this less than one hundred years ago.

I got two English Bibles with which I work every day, but the same story is written differently from one another.

Here is what I got from the Gideons' Bible in Matthew 13, 4. It is written: 'Jesus got up from supper and laid aside <u>his garments</u>; and taking a towel, he <u>girded</u> himself.'

Now John 13, 4 in the New International Bible. 'So Jesus got up from the meal, took off his <u>outer clothing</u>, and wrapped a towel around his waist.'

For this John it was supper time.

So, it is obvious they have changed one part of this verse, but they weren't smart enough to change the way this Jesus dressed up when he was done with their feet. See John 13, 12. 'When this Jesus had finished washing their feet, he put on his clothes and returned to his place.'

This is the same Jesus who could not keep his mouth shut when he was interrogated in this John; contrary to the true Christ, the true Messiah has done. Check it out in Matthew.

We have to understand here that Jesus was only wearing a robe and underwear; so if he took his clothes off he was completely naked, which I don't believe the true prophet Jesus did this.

If you want to know who was strong on the washing of feet go read 1 Timothy 5, 10.

See Genesis 9, 25. Noah cursed one of his grand-sons because his son saw his nakedness and he condemned him to slavery and Jesus would have undressed completely to be naked in front of his apostles??????

The same John who like I said before likes the naked men undressed also Peter. Of course if he could undress the Master why not undress the most considerate of all the apostles too, the captain? Read John 21, 7. 'Therefore the disciple whom Jesus loved (the favourite one according to himself as if he was the only one to be loved by Jesus) said to Peter, 'It is the Lord.' So when Simon Peter heard that it was the Lord he put his clothes back on, for <u>he was naked</u> and threw himself into the see.'

Him Peter, who didn't know how to swim. See Matthew 14, 30.

These are two unbelievable stories that you can find nowhere else than in this John. Like I said before; this John was put there to open the way for Paul just Like John the Baptist opened the way for Jesus. It is just a very bad imitation.

Paul, the spirit, the helper who was to come. See John 14, 16, 14, 26, 15, 26, 16, 7 and 16, 13. No where else in the whole Bible I could find the word helper. I found it five times in this John. The other apostles didn't mention this at all, because Jesus never talked to them about this one. The helper this John talked about is Paul, the devil himself.

Jesus said everything he could to his apostles and for sure we don't have everything that was said, but the beast couldn't have created all those religions without; it is sad to say but the beast couldn't do it without the word of God. In the same way the devil seduced and deceived Adam and Eve, he seduced and deceived the entire world with the story of Jesus. Only the beast had the desire and the power to do such a devilish thing.

See Matthew 24, 4. 'And Jesus answered and said to them, 'See to it that no one misleads you.' '

Jesus warned us alright, but he is crafty the enemy and most people would rather believe the lies than the truth. It is very sad though.

Of course the beast knows its end is coming with the truth being known in the whole world and it is not in a hurry for this to happen. The beast knows the truth and the scripture and this makes it tremble. The beast believes in it enough to kill everyone who talks about the truth and its sordid crimes are in some ways self-defence for its surviving. Kill to avoid destruction which will come anyway, this is its policy.

I have to say that I am happy to participate in its destruction. By killing the children of God the beast proves its identity. Do you see? The beast believes in God maybe more than most and is frightened to death just like my friend James; Jesus' brother said it in James 2, 19. 'You believe there is only one God. You do well; the demons also believe and shudder.'

They shudder being scared that their end is near and this is the reason for killing Jesus' disciples and the prophets; the ones who spread the word of God so dangerous to them.

CHAPTER 5

Not so long ago I thought the Catholic Church alone was the beast, but after more reflection and a deeper look on the activities and the politics of the protestant churches; I came to the conclusion that even if they protested some of the Catholics practices, like praying the Virgin Mary; they too are following Paul. In fact Pastor means the same thing than father, only the word has changed. Most of them too sanctify the first day of the week contrary to the law of God, contrary to the commandments, which is the exact reason for us to obtain eternal life according to Jesus himself. See Matthew 19, 17. 'But if you want to enter into life, keep the commandments.'

Most of the people who hunted down Louis Riel like an animal, the ones who put a price on his head, who condemned him to death were Protestants, some Christians and they were in the same boat than the Catholics.

According to the information I found the Anglican, the united Church and the Catholic Church were involved in the residential schools of the West and so was the Canadian Government of John A. MacDonald. They all participated to the torture in the massacres of the Métis and of the Natives children.

I just wonder how many of their parents who knew about the truth have been killed, which is the result of Louis Riel's efforts, betrayed unconsciously and involuntary by their children.

It would be very difficult today to get testimonies for what I'm saying in this book about this massacre, because the last witness was shut up many generations ago. Only the visions that come to me from God could be questioned. For sure there will be debates and criticisms and I have no doubt at all about this. Jesus told us not to worry about what to say that the Spirit of the Father will speak for us. See Matthew 10, 19. 'Do not worry about how or what you are to say; for it will be given to you in the hour what you are to say.'

When I started to write this book I had no idea of what I was going to say or rather I had very little. I'm up now to about one hundred pages and I still have no idea about what is coming next and neither where all this will end. I now though think it is time for another pretty song that I just love a lot and it is another proof that God is speaking to me. It's called;

The Last Warning.

Listen to this one great news sent to you today
To me it's the greatest; the Lord is in his way
He has made the universe, the earth and heavens
And all that you can see has been made by his hands.
'Many times I have showed you the mighty power
I have flooded the earth, but I have saved Noah.
When Abram the good man has pleaded for his friends
They got out of the towns, Sodom and Gomorrah.

Do you remember Joseph I sent to exile?
He was sold by his brothers, he was put in jail.
He was to save my people from the starvation
Of a deadly famine seven years duration.
And what to say of Moses drew out of water
To guide you to the crises and a lot of danger?
I told him all I wanted for you to know.
He carried all my commands down to you below.

The wisdom of Solomon, the strength of Samson
Can just not save your soul from the lake of fire.

Only Jesus the Saviour with his compassion
Left his beautiful home they took him for ransom.
I sent you my loved son, his life he sacrificed
He has done nothing wrong, yet he has paid the price
Now if you are telling Me this is not for you.
Just one more thing to say, I've done all I can do.

Now you are out of time and I am out of blood
Too many of my children have died for their God.
Many of Jesus good friends and his apostles.
And so many others died as his disciples.
Now it is time to crown my own beloved son.
He's going back to run everything I have done
Will you be lost forever or will you be saved?
This is what you should know before you hit the grave.'

Listen to this one great news sent to you today
To me it's the greatest; the Lord is in his way
He has made the universe, the earth and heavens
And all that you can see has been made by his hands.
Yes that all you can see has been made by his hands.

For the people who like to sing, this is an old time waltz.

Many people asked me why I do this things and why I write about the scriptures of the Bible. There is only one answer which comes to my mind and this is because I love God with all of my heart and my neighbour as myself and I want everybody to know what I know about the truth. So I share my knowledge the best way I know with as many people as possible and this includes the entire world; which brings me to another song a lot of people like.

I Love My Neighbour as Myself

Part sang

I love my neighbour as myself; which causes me
some problems
What can you do when you're turned down
trying to help someone?

Part spoken

I walked into a restaurant the other day and a
man said hi to me.
I said hi too and I told him to go ahead even
though I came in first.
He said; 'No, you go ahead, I have all day.'
I said ok then, I'll bet you this girl can serve two
coffees at the same time and she did.
So when came to pay, I paid for both and he
said; 'No, you don't buy me coffee.' Almost
in madness! 'You owe me nothing and I owe
nothing.'
And he put a toonie ($2) in the tray.
So I took a loonie ($1) and I gave it to him,
thinking; if you can't take it, it's because you
can't give.

Part sang

I love my neighbour as myself, which causes me
some problems

What can you do when you're turned down trying to help someone?

Second part spoken

There's a young woman whom I like who works in the same place and I saw her limping with sore feet.
I know she's working seven days a week trying to make ends meet.
So I wrote in a napkin that seeing her suffer is killing me and I put some money in it; asking her to buy a good pair of shoes, because I want her to be comfortable when she walks up to me table.
She brought it back all upset telling me that she couldn't take it. I felt so sad thinking; if you can't
take it, it's because you can't give.

Part sang

I love my neighbour as myself, which causes me some problems
What can you do when you're turned down trying to help someone?

3rd part spoken

A man whom I know came to fix my driveway the same day and he did a very good job. So I gave him a little more than he had expected.

Then he handed me back forty dollars, saying;
'It's more than I deserved.'
I took twenty dollars out of his hand telling him;
I'll share it with you if you like it better, but then
again, I couldn't help thinking; if you can't take
it, it's because you can't give.

Part sang

I love my neighbour as myself, which causes me
some problems
What can you do when you're turned down
trying to help someone?

4th part spoken

At the end of that day I was filled with sadness
thinking of Jesus who left everything behind to
give us the word of God, the God who talked
to him as he walked day by day! He gave much
more than I could ever give; by healing the sick,
bringing back to life and mainly by opening the
eyes of the blind!
Through all of his ministry he risked his life
every minute of every day until they took it.
How many still today say; thanks but no thanks?
I can't take it. They can't take it I think, because
they can't give.
Today someone gave me an extra dollar and
I knew it was from the heart. I gladly took it,
because I love to give.

Part sang

I love my neighbour as myself, which causes me
some problems
What can you do when you're turned down
trying to help someone? Trying to help someone.

I had a totally different song, which I call spiritual already
chosen to put on a Cd I was getting ready to record, but God
made me see these three events the same day, because I think
this was the message He wanted me to put with my other songs.
I'm sure this song will touch many people some day.

The man who came to fix my driveway had a totally
different idea in his mind when he offered me to do the job.
This is why he was a bit ashamed to take my money. The truth
was he wanted to play music with me. When I mentioned this
song to him, because he was concerned; he admitted then I was
right. He made many songs too, but almost all of them for the
Virgin Mary and this is the main reason we couldn't get along
very long. He has many idols and I only have one God. I have
absolutely nothing against Mary, the mother of Jesus; I simply
only want to let her have her rightful place. When I want to see
a doctor I don't go to his mother; I want to see the one who can
help me and fix my problem.

The young woman whom I like a lot was probably afraid
I tried to seduce her and who knows, maybe the gentleman
too. He kind of apologized and saluted me on his way out after
breakfast though.

Millions got caught by the liar concerning the one who was
a virgin before getting together with Joseph. If you read the
story very carefully you will understand first that Jesus was not
in a condition to speak or to make any recommendation when
he was hanging on the cross. Read Matthew 27, 55-56. 'Many
women were there looking on from a distance, who had followed
Jesus from Galilee to care for his needs. Among them were Mary

Magdalene and Mary the mother of James and Joseph and the mother of the sons of Zebedee.'

So, according to a true apostle, an apostle who has really spent time with Jesus and his mother Mary; it is not true the mother of Jesus was near the cross at the time of his death and neither was the true John who would have been crucified too if this had been the case.

Go read now John 19, 25-26 very carefully too, will you? 'But standing by the cross of Jesus were his mother and his mother's sister, Mary the wife of Clopas, and Mary Magdalene. When Jesus then saw his mother and the disciple whom he loved standing nearby, (as if this John was the only one to be loved by Jesus or as if Jesus had a man lover. Maybe the Jesus of this John was like this, but not the true Jesus, the son of God.) he said to his mother; 'Woman, behold, here's your son.' Then he said to his disciple; 'Behold, here's your mother.' From that hour the disciples took her into his own household.'

It is not surprising there are so many homosexuals and paedophiles within the clergy. I say this John is a terrible liar for more than one reason. First, every one of them who were friends with Jesus was in danger to be crucified with him that day; especially his disciples and his apostles who were all dispersed like the true story tells. See Matthew 26, 31. 'Then Jesus said to them; 'You will all fall away because of me this night, for it is written, 'I will strike down the shepherd and the sheep of the flock shall be scattered.' ' '

You can believe Jesus who said it and Matthew who wrote it; they were all scattered and there was no disciple near Jesus' cross that day around the time of his death and this was for a very good reason too. If they were near the cross they would all have been killed too; crucified with Jesus and the result would have been that we would have next to nothing from him now.

Yes, the disciples all fell that day, but I'm sure the all have repented too, because Jesus said they will be with him to judge the twelve tribes of Israel. It's written in Matthew 19, 28. The second thing that makes me believe this John is a liar is the fact that Jesus was way too much broken down to speak this long and if he did this he would have condemned to death the ones he loved. The ones who witnessed the death of Jesus if there are some from his disciples they saw him from a distance.

The story of Peter's denying of knowing Jesus is a proof they wanted to kill the Jesus' apostles too. If he didn't do what he did he wouldn't have carried the key of the kingdom of heaven very long and not very far.

We can read this story in Matthew 26, 69-75. Third, but not the least, Jesus' brothers were alive, so Mary, Jesus' mother had still a lot of family and she had no need at all that one disciple take her to his place. They were taking care of their parents in those days and I believe the holy family could do just this. They were born with their parents and their parents were dying with their children back then.

Finally if Jesus would have really said these things to John and to his mother, Matthew would have heard about it and he too would have talked about it.

Then this story brings me to the story of the two criminals who were hanged beside Jesus. This is another story, this one in Luke which contradicts the same story in Matthew. See what it said in Luke 23, 43. 'And he said to him, 'Truly I say to you, today you shall be with me in paradise.' '

Now just compare this with Matthew 27, 44. 'The robbers who had been crucified with him (Jesus) were also insulting him with the same words.'

When I remember my young schools days the teachers were asking us to analyze the words and the phrases. I guess I didn't lose all of it yet.

How can we believe this story from Luke when it is written somewhere else in the New Testament that Jesus didn't go up to his Father yet and this only happened like forty days after his resurrection?

See John 20, 17. 'Jesus said to her, 'Stop clinging to me, (in French he said, 'don't touch me') I have not yet ascended to the Father.' '

Now this was like three days after Jesus' death.

Now, if I recapitulate all this I get a stew for cats.

Matthew 27, 44, the two robbers were insulting Jesus the same way the soldiers were doing.

Luke 23, 43, Jesus said to one of them; <u>today</u> you will be in paradise with me.

John 20, 17, no one can touch Jesus because he didn't go back to his Father yet, 4 days later.

John 20, 27, Jesus would have told Thomas to touch his injuries a couple of days later. So the holy ladies who follow him through out his ministry couldn't touch him, but one of his disciples who had a hard time believing in his resurrection could?????????

Jesus told us that we will recognize the tree by its fruits, the liar by his lies, but at the risk of repeating myself; I really don't believe this John is the John of Jesus, but rather the John of Paul, meaning an impostor.

Luke too was Paul's best friend. I also believe the Mark of the gospels is the Mark of Paul. Now you are worn and it's up to you to be careful when you read. More than ninety per cent of the New Testament is from Paul and company. The weeds among the wheat! The lawless infiltrated the scriptures, exactly there where he could do the most wrong, the most damages and he didn't miss his shot.

I think that Paul's best description is in Daniel and so are many other good messages. See Daniel 11, 37. 'He will show no regard for the gods of his fathers or for the one desired by women, nor will he regard any god, but will exalt himself above them all.'

We can certainly say that Paul is not the one the most liked by women; especially when he said they have to keep their mouth shut in the assemblies. This kind of proved he didn't know them very well. We have seen also that Paul didn't have too much regard for the judge he had to face at his trial. See Acts 23, 3.

The end will come when this book, the truth, the Jesus' messages will be known in the entire world and the beast knows it and this is why it will do anything and everything to stop this work of mine. For sure even many people who love God will destroy some of my books too; especially before they really understand they were seduced by the liar.

I'm asking them to think twice before destroying maybe the only chance they have to get their eyes opened.

I personally don't know anyone else in the world who dare writing this way about the weeds of the Bible and when I'll be gone I won't be able to do it anymore and I don't want the truth to be killed with me. The truth is a precious stone, a pearl of great value and you cannot find too many in a life time.

It is a sure thing the ones who follow the churches don't have anything to fear from the beast, but everything to fear from God. The last person with whom I discussed these matters doesn't believe that Jesus is against religions; so I will expose a few passages that prove it.

One I already mentioned is in Matthew 23, 8-10. Jesus tells his disciples not to call anyone on earth father, Rabbi or even director. When Jesus gave his instructions to his disciples he mentioned to them they will be flogged in the synagogues, meaning; stay away from these places. This is in Matthew 10, 17. I'm sure I would be mistreated in the Christian churches too. I already have.

They would certainly not let me preach against their politics! Jesus said to go find a deserving home worthy of the word of God and to stay there until leaving this town. This is certainly not in a Christian church. This is written in Matthew 10, 11.

Jesus said the scribes, the Pharisees, the leaders of churches were hypocrites and they were shutting down the kingdom of heaven in people's face. It is written in Matthew 23, 13.

Jesus said these hypocrites were devouring the widows' homes and they were for a pretence making long prayers; and therefore they will receive greater condemnation. This is written in Matthew 23, 14.

Jesus said these hypocrites, these leaders, were travelling the seas and land to make one proselyte and when he became one; they make him a son of hell twice as much as they are. This is in Matthew 23, 15.

Jesus said many times these church's leaders were blind. See Matthew 23, 16-22.

Jesus said earlier they were blind guides of the blind. See Matthew 15, 14.

Jesus said they were neglecting the most important, love, justice and mercy, see Matthew 23, 23.

Jesus said they look clean on the outside but they were full of hypocrisy and lawlessness in the inside. See Matthew 23, 28. This is what I say too.

Jesus said they were killing the prophets and the disciples of God. It's written in Matthew 23, 30-31. Am I wrong by saying the same thing Jesus said?

Jesus said they are serpents, brood of vipers and he asked how they could escape the sentence of hell. See Matthew 23, 33.

Jesus said God send them prophets and disciples, wise men, scribes, some of them they kill and crucify, others they scourge in their churches and persecute from city to city. Now they go from province to province too. See Matthew 23, 34.

We also know who were executing by crucifixion, don't we?

Jesus said not to bring money in our belts, that the worker deserves his stay. It is written in Matthew 10, 9.

Jesus said we will be persecuted when we'll speak about the word of God and how many people like Louis Riel and Jesus were assassinated because of it?

Jesus repeated again and again that the leaders of the churches were hypocrites and blind! It is not for the sins of the world that Jesus was murdered, but rather because he told them he was the son of God and also he told them what he thought of them. See John 19, 7. 'The Jews answered him, 'We have a law and by that law he ought to die because he made himself out to be the son of God.' '

I could get kill for this reason too, because I say the same thing.

John the Baptist was also killed because he dared telling the truth.

I tell the truth too, but mainly I write it; knowing very well the words pass but the writing stays. At least this is what they say. I think God will allow the ones He wants to save to read and to understand what I'm writing; what is true and I hope they will be careful and simple enough to stay alive long enough to instruct others.

News travel at the speed of the light and the controversies do even faster than the rest with the Internet and the television nowadays. I only hope that once my book is out on the market I won't be the only one to spread the truth, but my biggest wish would be that I can make disciples from all the nations like Jesus asked me to do and then there will be enough of them; so the truth will never be choked again like it has been.

Everyone who loves God with all their heart, their soul and mind would surely end up understanding that all I do is telling the truth and it can be verify if only people bother to check it out except a few things maybe like my visions and my dreams! I can assure you though that the beast will go wild when it hears about this and this until it will be locked up for one thousand years. Although this beast will have a lot of time to do a lot of damages; especially to the Jesus' disciples, the God's elects and it's because of them these times will be cut short. You can read this in Matthew 24, 22.

Can we only imagine times and events worst than we already had like the world war two?

There is a good reason why Jesus told us not to look behind and not to return to take a coat. People who don't accept the truth will be invited to take the mark of the beast. They will then face the eternal sentence of hell; which is thousands of times worst than death and the suffering of the human body (torture). Be ready to die for a good living rather than live for death. Jesus told us and you can read it in Matthew 10, 39 and in Matthew 16, 25. 'He who has found his life will lose it, and he who has lost his life for my sake will find it.'

I would like to translate this a bit more completely.

'The one who would save his life by rebuking the word of God will lose it and the one who lose his life for the sake of the word of God will find it.' Eternal life.

Don't you go cry the life of Louis Riel, because he got his life back; word of Jesus and you can trust his word. I am sure Louis Riel's fate is more enjoyable than the ones responsible for his death. I'm sure too that Louis Riel sits at the same table than Jesus. See Matthew 8, 11. 'I say to you that many will come from east and west and recline at the table with Abraham, Isaac and Jacob in the kingdom of heaven.'

We can take the example from Jesus, Louis Riel and the Jews who were brought to the gas chambers during the 1939-44 war. See Isaiah 53, 7. 'He was oppressed and he was afflicted, yet he did not open his mouth; <u>like</u> a lamb (not as a lamb) that is led to slaughter and <u>like</u> a sheep (not as a sheep) that is silent before its shearers, he did not open his mouth.'

The people of Israel who is also the son of God was brought to the gas chambers without saying a word, without open their mouth, as if they knew it was no use and no point giving to the sons of the devil any enjoyment of any kind.

See what it is written in Hosea 11, 1. 'When Israel was a youth I loved him, and out of Egypt I called my son.' See also Matthew 2, 15.

So, just like I underlined above Jesus kept his mouth shut like a lamb and like a sheep before death, but he was not a lamb and neither a sheep. Jesus is not an animal like the Christians made him to be. The Christians with their zeal for the beast have made Jesus, the Saviour, the son of God, the one they say is God made man an animal, a lamb. What kind of consideration this is for the Saviour? See John 1, 29 and John 1, 36. 'And he looked at Jesus as he walked and said; "Behold, the Lamb of God!"'

When the time will come for you to be oppressed and afflicted my brothers and sisters in Jesus, I advise you to do just the same; keep your mouth shut when you are accused. I'm not talking here about the chances you'll have to testify the truth before the kings or judges without swearing but when the whole world will be upside down and there will be no way out for you.

See Matthew 10, 18-20. 'And you will even be brought before governors and kings for the sake of the word of God as a testimony to them and to the gentiles. But when they hand you over, do not worry about how or what you are to say; for it will be given to you in that hour what you are to say. For it is not you who speaks, but it is the Spirit of your Father who speaks in you.'

This is another proof that God, the Father speaks to us, to his children; so this shouldn't be this surprising to you what I'm writing in this book.

It is also the Spirit of my Father who speaks in this book and inspired me it. People who will reject it will reject the truth and will reject the Father. It would be good for you Christians of the entire world to remember what Jesus told Peter; which is written in Matthew 18, 18 and in Matthew 16, 19. 'I will give you the keys of the kingdom of heaven and what ever you bind on earth shall been bound in heaven and what ever you loose on earth shall have been loosed in heaven.'

So don't make too many faces to the Jesus' disciples, would you? I advise you to make friends with them (the disciples) and to learn from them for your own sake and for your own salvation.

If you on the contrary betray them, well, your life doesn't even worth living; you are just like Judas who betrayed Jesus and about whom it was said it would have been better for him if he wasn't born. See Matthew 26, 24. "But woe to this man by whom the Son of Man is betrayed! It would have been good for this man if he had not been born.'

This would be very sad, but this is the way it is.

I know it is shocking finding out we were lied to, but it is even worst to continue living in this lie once you have discovered the truth, because then; you will have no more excuse. If only you could understand the joy to see and to know the kingdom of heaven; you would not waste a single second.

Here I have another proof the kingdom of heaven is here on earth. Look in Matthew 11, 12. 'From the days of John the Baptist until now the kingdom of heaven suffers violence, and violent men take it by force.'

Believe it or not, but the violent men are not able to take over the kingdom of God. Look also in Matthew 12, 28. 'Then the kingdom of God has come upon you.'

Yes, the word of God came upon men and men seem to take pleasure in rejecting it just like twenty-five thousands of them did it at mount Sinai and this after seeing all the marvellous wonders God has done for them.

You might ask how come I know all these things. The answer is in Matthew 13, 11. 'Jesus answered them, 'To you it has been granted to know the mysteries of the kingdom of heaven, but to them it has not been granted.' '

Here we are; many mysteries are not mysteries to me anymore.

There is another mystery that I brought light on without searching too much. This is the one where Jesus said to one of his disciples to leave the dead bury the dead and to follow him. See Matthew 8, 21-22. 'Another of the disciples said to Jesus; 'Lord, permit me first to go and bury my father.' But Jesus said to him; 'Follow me and allow the dead to bury their own dead.' '

What do you get out of this message? I'm going to give you some time to think about this one and I'll tell you a bit later what I found. You'll find my answers in a few pages farther.

God speaks to me and I made many songs from his messages and here is another one called;

You Told Me Lord

You told me oh my Lord; You brought to us the sword,
The kingdom of heaven belongs to your children.
You made beautiful things, for You I'll be pleading.
I found You amazing and for You I will sing.

You are the Father of the heavens and the earth.
You know all the secrets of the earth and the sea.
Some want to take over what You created first.
Only You knows how to control the universe.

Only You who can change our heart and our thoughts.
What can I do for You? For You I love so much.
From your word came my faith, now I do know my fate.
For You I want to sing, the Master of all things.

You are the Father of the heavens and the earth.
You know all the secrets of the earth and the sea.
Some want to take over what You created first.
Only You knows how to control the universe.

You showed me oh my Lord that life is not a game.
Many mock you my Lord, everywhere is the shame.
Everything goes down hill, enough to make me ill.
Sing is my destiny for the eternity.

You are the Father of the heavens and the earth.
You know all the secrets of the earth and the sea.
Some want to take over what You created first.
Only You knows how to control the universe.
Only You knows how to control the universe.

When we pay attention at what we read and we look for the truth like Jesus told us to do, because the truth is hidden just like he told us in the parable of the weeds; then we find a lot of interesting things. We can find for one thing the truth is not this easy to find among the lies in big quantity. Do I need to tell you that the New Testament is from Paul at 90-95 per cent? You can verify this for yourselves. Let me tell you that Luke, Mark and John are Paul's disciples. Most of the writings in Peter are also from Paul! 99 per cent of the Acts of the apostles are about Paul. Everything from Romans to the end of Hebrews is from

Paul! The revelation is almost completely from the John of Paul and his seven churches. This makes a lot of weeds and very little wheat, many lies and very little of the truth. No wonder Jesus told us to look for the truth, to be careful when we read. He knew very well the beast would do everything possible to hide the truth from us and do everything it can to deceive us. See Matthew 7, 7. 'Ask and it will be given to you; <u>seek and you will find</u>, knock and it will be opened to you.'

He told us too in Matthew 12, 33 that we will recognize the tree by its fruits. This too was for a very good reason. Once we have found a bunch of things, a bunch of lies, a bunch of contradictions, things which are contrary to the teaching of Jesus, contrary or opposed to the law of God; then we know whom we are facing. Jesus told us too this was the devil. See Matthew 13, 39. 'The enemy who sowed them is the devil.'

I found more than five hundred bad fruits in the New Testament and believe me they are not from Jesus or from one of his disciples. Most of the lies and contradictions I found are exposed in my second book called; The True Face of The Antichrist. There is in this book enough information to give anyone enough knowledge to cause someone to be killed. There is in this book more material than most people can take in one shot; especially for the ones who believe in their religion like they should believe in God and believe in their pastors and in the Bible thinking that it is the absolute truth.

There is one thing Louis Riel had and I don't and this is people who were ready to fight for him. I feel alone in the world but I know God is with me and I hope He will send me his angels to protect me when I need. If there are other disciples in the world at this time I didn't heard about them. I know too that nothing will happen to me that God Himself will not allow. See Matthew 10, 30. 'But the very hairs of your head are all numbered.'

I can assure you that God spent a lot of time over my head, because I lost most of my hairs. Another thing is sure and this is I couldn't count them all myself and neither count the piece of sand of the sea. I can't even count all of the benedictions that come my way and many of them I don't even know about. I'm not sure either if I will ever meet with another disciple, but I sure hope I will in my passage on earth. I know I will meet with someone who pretends to be.

It was said by I don't know whom that a new Bible will be written before the end of the age, but be assure of one thing, it is not the lies that will disappear from the book, but most of the truth like; don't call anyone on earth father and Matthew 5, 17-18. I even think Matthew might disappear completely, because it contains ninety per cent of the truth of the New Testament.

I would like to give you an example of what I mean by this. Take John 13, 4. 'Jesus got up from supper and laid aside his <u>garments</u> and taking a towel, he <u>girded himself.</u>'

All Jesus was wearing are a robe and an underwear. So Jesus would have gotten completely naked in front of his apostles to wash his disciples' feet, girded himself with a towel and then got naked again by taking this towel off to wipe his disciples' feet. In the new Bibles Jesus takes his <u>outer garment</u> off, but when he dressed himself he put <u>his garments</u> on and this is in John 13, 12. This is a very small detail, but it shows that when someone with some influence wants to change the scripture he can when something doesn't make sense to him. The person responsible for the change was not bright enough to make the change in both places. This must have frustrated Paul's disciples not to have Jesus naked anymore like they like it. Personally I don't believe in this story at all. I don't believe either in the story of the water changed for wine in John 2, 1-12 and this for several reasons.

Jesus, the son of God, the one they say is God would have changed from one hundred and twenty gallons to one hundred and eighty gallons of water in strong wine for a crowd that was already drunk. Besides, Jesus who was gentle and humble in heart, (Matthew 11, 29) would have been nothing less than rude to his mother by telling her more or less to mind her own business. Read John 2, 4. On top of that Jesus' mother didn't know that Jesus could do some miracles simply because he didn't make any by that time.

Today I found another one a bit ridiculous, part of it anyway and it is in Luke 2, 16-19. 'But you will be betrayed even by parents and brothers and relatives and friends, and they will put some of you to death and you will be hated by all because of my name. Yet <u>not a hair of your head will perish</u>.'

This is quite different than having your hairs being all numbered. John the Baptist who had his head cut off; did he worried about his hairs?

This subject of losing hairs is totally out of context over here. Go tell someone he's going to die to see if he's going to worry about his hairs.

Now, to come back on the dead burying the dead; see what I found on this subject. For sure the dead doesn't come out of his coffin to bury another dead, but it is probably what the church people do best, to bury the dead. Leave the dead bury the dead means let the sinners bury the cadavers.

'You follow me.' Means Jesus needed him, a sinless disciple. It also means Jesus was in a hurry enough not to let this man go bury his dad and what he had to do was more important. It also means there is nothing else you can do for the dead and neither could Jesus and he too had better things to do.

I'm pretty sure Louis Riel had found most of these things, but there was no way in his time he could publish his findings at the speed of the light like we can today. With a bit of luck and yet I'll be very lucky if I can publish my work before the beast destroy it. Besides, I had the luck to read the story of Louis Riel; which is for me a very nice warning on top of the warnings I received from Jesus as far as carefulness is concerned.

This allows me to write many pages before they could find me anyway. There is one thing Louis Riel said at his trial that help me to understand a lot and this is when he said: 'So many things to say and so little time to say it.'

By limiting myself in my efforts to convince people to look at the truth this allowed me to write many books and I'm pretty sure that in time God will allow me to publish them and to spread the truth in the whole world.

Only then, when all the nations know about it will come the end of the reign of the devil, the reign of the beast. See Matthew 24, 14. 'The gospel of the kingdom of heaven shall be preached in the whole world as a testimony to all the nations and then the end will come.'

I personally just started this movement of novelty, this movement of freshness, but I will need thousands of other disciples to complete the task and I sure hope they will answer the call.

For sure the beast is not in a hurry for this to happen and it does everything in its power to slow down the process. Who has interest to stop the truth being spread everywhere in the world? Did you realize these were all of the religions of the world with their satanic business?

I never heard anyone preach the kingdom of heaven like I do, beside Jesus of course and I'm collecting my old aged pension. I might just be the only one in many years to do it. All I can say is I have some dough on the boards. I just hope I can multiply bread like Jesus was doing. The only way I can do this is by having my books on the market and having the truth to fall in some hears of people who love God with all their heart, their soul and mind. One thing is sure is I am totally powerless in controlling the destiny of my books when they're out of my hands. I only hope they cross the world like a hurricane and leave some prints everywhere on their passageway. I know the beast will do what James, Jesus' brother said about the demons in James 2, 19. 'You believe that there is only one God, you do well; the demons also believe that and <u>they shudder</u>.'

They will kill the Jesus' disciples hoping to stretch their time on earth, but this time this will be in vain, because it is written their end will come for them. When Jesus said just before going to his Father he will be with us always to the end of the age; he knew that even with all its efforts the beast won't be able to eliminate the truth completely, all the word of God. The beast didn't eliminate the truth, but it did like the crafty serpent in the Garden of Eden did; it twisted the truth to deceive the world. This is what the devil is doing from the beginning. See Genesis 3, 1-5. God said one thing, but the devil manipulated the truth to deceive Adam and Eve.

God said the law will always be and Jesus said that not even a single letter will disappear from the law, but the devil said the whole law doesn't exist anymore and we're not under the law anymore but under the grace by faith. The routine of the devil is still the same; which should in principal alert us against him, but unfortunately too many people didn't take this seriously enough and they got caught in the devil's trap.

Let me remind you of what the devil did in the Garden of Eden to Adam and Eve. God said not to touch the tree of Good and evil and if they do surely they will die. What did the devil do? He said they won't die but they will be like God; meaning they will not die but they will know good and evil. The exact same thing happened with the law of God. Only now if you read up to these lines you are just like me; you know where the devil put his venom.

Don't you go think I was born with this information! I was caught in his trap for a time too, but I'm very glad God delivered me from evil and I am very thankful to Him for opening my eyes. I appreciate too the fact He entrusted in me this gigantic work which is to open the eyes of the rest of the world and this I cannot do alone. The beast will probably shorten my life and send me in the other world where I will be with Jesus, Abraham, Isaac, Jacob, Louis Riel and many more.

Before finishing, I would like to bring some light about what is written in Matthew 10, 39. 'He who has found his life will lose it and who has lost his life for my sake will find it.'

If I translate this in our language it would give you this; when the beast will ask you on which side you are; are you on Jesus' side or on the religion side? If you say on the religion side to save your life; then you'll be lost and if you say on Jesus' side, you might die, but you will be alive for the eternity and you will join me at the same table with Jesus to celebrate our victory.

The same thing is written in Matthew 16, 25. 'For whoever wishes to save his life will lose it, but whoever loses his life for my sake <u>will find it</u>.'

Now just try to see the difference of what is written in Mark 8, 35, because there is a little deviation. 'For whoever wishes to save his life will lose it, but whoever loses his life for my sake and the gospel's <u>will save it</u>.'

Here it is written whoever loses his life for Jesus' sake <u>will save it</u>. This is false. You cannot lose your life and save it, but if you lose it for the word of God then you can find it like Jesus said in Matthew and this will be eternal life. It is just a small detail, but a very big difference.

In Luke 9, 24 it is basically the same thing than in Mark 8, 35. 'For whoever wishes to save his life will lose it, but whoever loses his life for my sake, he is the one who <u>will save it</u>.'

Of course it is false here too. There is a very big difference between save his life and get it back. There is nothing wrong by wanted to save your life. Peter did it and so did Jesus when he fled the ones who wanted to catch him to kill him. Jesus did just this almost continually for the three years of his ministry.

In Luke 17, 33 it is still a bit different. 'Whoever seeks to keep his life will lose it and whoever loses his life will preserve it.'

Again there is nothing wrong by seeking to keep your life. What is wrong is to rebuke the word of God and if we do it to save our life, then this is cowardliness. I pray God to give me the strength to be strong enough when ever this happens. If Peter who carried the keys of the kingdom of heaven was afraid to die the day he denied knowing Jesus; don't you think you'll be much better.

Although in Peter's case it was the most necessary and it was God who allowed this to happen; so we can get his word today. As I have already said if the apostles didn't all flee that day God would have had to start all over and rise up another prophet like Moses and Jesus. See Deuteronomy 18, 18. See also Isaiah 53.

But the worst about this message is in John 12, 25. 'He who loves his life loses it, and he who hates his life in this world will keep it to life eternal.'

As if loving you life is something wrong and hating it is a way to get eternal life. I just don't know where this John took his information, but the very word hate should be in a disciple's mouth only to describe sin and evil. Jesus didn't say this person would save his life, but he will find it, which is not quite the same thing. Don't forget to meditate about Genesis 3.

I wish you the very best of luck in the world and mainly the strength to resist evil, to resist the beast and mainly not to be afraid to be free from the bad of this world. I would like though to add a letter I called: If you knew. This letter is from a Jesus' disciple to the entire world. So, I personally give the permission to everyone who would like to make a good action with this letter; this means in the unique goal to make the truth know to others to make as many copies as you think it is necessary.

If you knew?

It is not easy to decide where to begin; for there are so many lies and contradictions in the scriptures for the ones who want to see them of course. I will do my very best to expose a few of them which are susceptible to touch you or to open your eyes, something Jesus really like to do.

He said in Matthew 13, 25; 'But while everyone was sleeping, his enemy (and he said this was the devil) came and sowed the lies among the truth.'

The truth Jesus himself was seeding.

They are there those lies and I am sure you will see them too; if only you make an effort to look. No matter what I say, but him, Jesus, listen to him as God Himself asked you to do. See Matthew 17, 5.

There are there those lies and contradictions and some of them are big and some of them are very obvious. Take for example John 3, 16, it is written; 'For God so loved the world.'

Well, God so loved the world He asked his disciples to withdraw from it, not to live in the world. He basically said the world is the way to hell. I personally know the world is the kingdom of the devil and you have the proof in Matthew 4, 8-9. 'Again the devil took Jesus to a very high mountain and showed him all the kingdoms of the world and their glory; and he said to him, "All these things I will give you, if you fall down and worship me." '

We cannot give what we don't own.

It is said in the same verse John 3, 16 that God gave his one and only son; which would mean Jesus was his first born. It is said in Luke 3, 38 that Adam is also the son of God and the first one also. It is written that Jesus is the only son and not me, but the Bible proves otherwise. This is a lot in only one verse, but there is more.

Now it is written in Genesis 6, 1- 2; 'When men began to increase in number on the earth, and daughters were born to them, <u>the sons of God</u> saw that the daughters of men were beautiful, and they married any of them they chose.'

So according to this, there were more sons of God. So, it is not true Jesus is God's only son. Take a look also in Deuteronomy 32, 19. 'The Lord saw this and rejected them because He was angered by his <u>sons and daughters</u>.'

His sons and daughters; these were certainly not Jesus.

So according to these words from the Bible it is not true that Jesus is God's only son. In fact I know I am the son of God too because I do his will.

According to the Christian's believes and teaching I am God's brother, because they say Jesus is God became man and the same Jesus said the one who does the will of his Father in heaven is his brother, his sister and his mother. Look in Matthew 12, 50.

You most likely heard before that Jesus was God made man.

But let's go back to John 3, 16. According to this God would have sacrificed is first born, because it is said he is the only one. Go read 2 Kings 16, 3. 'He walked in the ways of Israel and even <u>sacrificed his son</u> in the fire following the <u>detestable ways</u> of the nations the Lord had driven out before the Israelites.'

God would have chased some nations in front of the people of Israel because they were offering their sons in sacrifice and according to this John He would have done the same thing?????????? Please?

And for what? To save the children of the devil, the sinners. Look in 1 John 3, 6-10.

I will tell you what is the truth and you can reed it in Deuteronomy 18, 18. 'I will raise up from them a prophet like you (Moses) from among their brothers, I will put my words in his mouth, and he will tell them everything I command him.'

This is what Jesus was sent for and this is what he did, to preach to us, to tell us what to do to be saved and what Jesus told us? Look in Matthew 4, 17. 'Repent for the kingdom of heaven is near.'

This is the truth either you want to believe it or not. Turn to God, not to anyone else. When did you hear Jesus say pray Marie or Joseph or any mortal? He didn't even say to pray Jesus, but he said to pray the Father in heaven. See Matthew 6, 9-14.

When you pray anyone else you pray the dead and it is an insult to God. It is impossible to men to live without sin, but with God everything is possible.

When Jesus said to the adulteress, 'I don't condemn you,' he also said something else very important and this was; 'Go now and live your life off sin.'

Jesus said it many times and this is the way to be saved and if you do sin; God will forgive you as long as you truly repent and turn away from your sin. See John 5, 14 and 8, 11. Jesus wouldn't have said this if it was impossible. There is a very important message in Matthew 24, 15. 'So when you see in the holy place (in the Holy Bible) the abomination that causes desolation, may the reader be careful when he reads.'

This is what I ask you to do too; not only to be careful of what you read, but to be careful to whom you talk to, because the beast is still killing the disciples of Jesus and they still say they are crazy.

There is another abomination I would like to talk to you about. You can find it in Matthew 1, 18. 'She was found to be with child through the <u>Holy Spirit</u>.'

That it was the will of God or the will of his Spirit for Jesus, the Saviour to be born from a young girl who was a virgin of fourteen before she went with Joseph; this I have no problem at all believing in. But to say that she got pregnant from the Holy Spirit the same way the pretty women did by the sons of God in the time of Noah is to say probably the worst abomination ever.

Was this the same Holy Spirit that was not yet in the world? According to John 14, 16, 14, 26, 15, 26, 16, 7, 16, 13 and Aces 2, 4. According to this John Jesus was to send the Holy Spirit down as soon as he was going to be with his Father in heaven. When we know that God was so mad when his angels, his sons took the pretty girls in the time of Noah; that He almost destroyed the whole earth and all life that was on it, including people and He would have done the same thing to get Marie, mother of Jesus pregnant. It is simply a total none sense. Look again at Genesis 6, 1-7.

If I understand well here, the sons of God, (The spirits or bad angels if you like it better) had sexual desires. It is possible to talk about these things today because the knowledge has increased. See Daniel 12, 4; 'Many will go here and there to increase knowledge.'

This is what I'm doing. We don't need to be a genius or a scientist to know nowadays and to witness this phenomenal truth.

My father and his cousin were looking in the stumps to find babies at the age of twelve. This is what they were told the babies come from in the year of 1922. Today a two years old child knows better. Yes, the knowledge has increased.

It is true there are some things that are hard to understand, but there are others that are very simple and easy.

Now, since the knowledge has increased this much my hope is that people of nowadays can understand that if God was mad enough to destroy just about everything and everyone who lived on the earth, because his sons, his angels were making children to the pretty daughters of men; it seems to me unlikely He would have done the same thing to get Mary, the mother of Jesus pregnant.

I know there are things that are hard to understand in the scriptures mainly because of the lies and the contradictions that were put in them by the evil one, but then there are others that are easy to comprehend.

Take for example the Paul's rapture. See 1 Thessalonians 4, 16-17. 'For the Lord himself will come down from heaven, with a loud command, with the voice of the archangel and with the trumpet call of God, and the <u>dead in Christ</u> will rise first. After that, <u>we</u> (Paul and his gang) who are still alive and are left will be caught up together with them (the dead in Christ) in the clouds to meet the Lord in the air. And so we will be with the lord forever.'

There he is; the bad bird will be caught in the air with the dead in Christ. For one thing, we are not dead in Christ, but we are alive. It is though up to you to be caught in the air with him and his followers.

Let me tell you now what Jesus said. See Matthew 13, 41-43. 'The <u>Son of Man</u> (means a prophet, not God) will send out his angels, and they will weed out of his Kingdom (means on earth) everything that causes sin and all who do evil. They will throw them into the fiery furnace, where there will be weeping and gnashing of teeth.'

Then me and the righteous that followed and follows Jesus will shine like the sun in the kingdom of our Father. He, who has ears, let him hear.

Do you want to shine like the sun in the kingdom of God with me or be caught up in the air and be thrown in the fiery furnace with Paul and his followers?

Paul said it himself he was taking away and now you know the rest.

Then it is proven that the ones who are dead in Christ are lost like the ones that Paul said he will be with. See 1 Corinthians 15, 18. 'Then those also who have fallen asleep in christ have perished.'

Here we are, the letters to the Corinthians are from Paul and so are the letters to the Thessalonians. Paul said it himself he is lost and he did everything in his power to take along with him as many people as possible. According to the way some members of my own family follow Paul I can tell Paul succeeded too.

It is up to you to decide if you want to be taken away also. It is written in Matthew 24, 37, word of Jesus that what happened in the time of Noah will happen again at the end time. What happened at the time of Noah is the bad people were taken away. Paul who said he will be taken away already pronounced his judgement.

See Matthew 24, 37-39. 'For the coming of the Son of Man will be just like the days of Noah. For as in those days before the flood they were eating and drinking, marrying and giving in marriage until Noah entered the ark, and they did not understand until the flood came and <u>took them all away</u>, so will the coming of the Son of Man be.'

It was said by Paul and company that Jesus died for our sins. Personally I think if someone who would give his life for our sins it would have to be the devil, he likes them. When it comes to Jesus he said that if we follow him (the word of God) we would never die; that we will have eternal life. This also means Jesus is still alive. He told us also what he would do with the one who keeps sinning. See Matthew 7, 23 'Then I will tell them plainly, I never knew you. Away from me you evildoers!' (sinners)

Jesus repeats the same message when he talks about the judgement of the nations. See Matthew 25, 31-46.

This is what he said also in the explanation of the parable of the weeds. Do you still feel like saying: 'We all have sins?' See Matthew 13, 41.

If you live in sins you are the son of the devil. See 1 John 3, 8. 'The one who practices sin is from the devil.'

I will end with some different messages, some are from Jesus and the others one are from Paul.

Jesus told us in Matthew 5, 17-18. 'Do not think that I have come to abolish the Law or the prophets, I have not come to abolish them but to fulfill them, I tell you the truth, until heaven and earth disappear, not the smallest letter, not the least stroke of a pen, will by any means disappear from the Law.'

God said, Jeremiah 31, 36. 'Only if these decrees vanish from my sight declares the Lord will the descendants of Israel ever cease to be a nation before Me.'

Now I don't know if you are blind enough not to see the earth and heaven or yet not to see the nation of Israel still exists, but the truth is they're still all there. On the other hand there is Paul who said the Law is gone, disappeared. See Galatians 3, 25; 'We are no longer under the supervision of the Law.'

See also Ephesians 2, 15. 'By abolishing in his flesh the Law with its commandments and regulations.'

'There is another one I call a terrible if not the worst abomination in the Bible. We all know the goal of the devil is to condemn everybody. Go read Paul in Hebrews 6, 4. 'It is impossible for those who have once been enlightened, (like the apostles) who have tasted the heavenly gift, (like the Jesus' apostles) who have shared in the Holy Spirit (like the apostles) who have tasted the goodness of the word of God and the power of the coming age, (like the apostles) If they fall away, (like the apostles) to be brought back to repentance, because, to their lost they are crucifying the son of God all over again.'

Now if it is impossible for the Jesus' disciples to be saved, no one can be, but here what Jesus said to his apostles. Matthew 19, 27. 'Jesus said to them, I tell you the truth, at the renewal of all things, when the Son of Man sits on his glorious throne, you who have followed me will also sit on twelve thrones, judging the twelve tribes of Israel.'

Check it out yourself and see Jesus in Matthew 5, 17-18. 'Do not think that I have come to abolish the Law or the prophets, I have not come to abolish them but to fulfill them, I tell you the truth, until heaven and earth disappear, not the smallest letter, not the least stroke of a pen, will by any means disappear from the Law.'

Now, can you compare this to Paul in Romans 10, 4. 'Christ is the end of the Law, so that there may be righteousness for everyone who believes.' (This is including the demons according to Paul)

There is a liar, but this is not Jesus and neither Matthew.

Here is a bit of homework for you.

See Jesus in Matthew 11, 19 versus Paul in Galatians 2, 16.

Jesus in Matthew 10, 42.

Jesus in Matthew 16, 27.

James 2, 14-24. And many more.

I'm going to let you digest all this, because I know this is not going to be easy for everybody. On the other hand if you want to get some more just know I got another five hundred and more.

Remember I worn you to be careful to whom you talk to. Louis Riel confided in his so called friends, a bishop and many priests and he died young, but not before being locked up for three years in St-Jean de Dieu, an asylum in East Montreal on a pretext to protect and hide him from persecution. He was accused of treason against the state, but in reality it was against the Catholic Church and Christianity in general, but it was not the church of Jesus-Christ. The church of Jesus would not have him killed or condemned him to death.

If you talk to someone who have a business like a church to protect or to defend don't expect to be welcome, neither you nor the word of God. Jesus too worn us. See Matthew 10, 16. 'I am sending you out like sheep among wolves; so be shrewd as snakes and innocent as doves.'

To be shrewd as snakes it is not to go yell on the roofs what you know now; so be innocent as doves and lower the tone and tell others carefully.

It is serious, be careful. Remember though that the work for God is never lost.

The last time I had a message from God it was in a dream as it happened most of the time. The message was to let you know my knowledge about these things.

The dream!

I was crying and I told God there was no point telling anyone about all this, because nobody, but nobody listen to what I have to say and everybody argues the truth. He told me then: 'You don't have to worry about this at all. All I ask you is to tell them either they listen to you or not or what they think or say; this way no one will be able to blame Me. They will know I sent them someone to wake them up, to open their eyes.'

End of the dream! It was for me the most peaceful message I have ever received from Him, but it was also a message that told me to do it.

If you're ever afraid to lose your mind or anyone accuses you of this you can answer this; it is better to lose an eye or a hand than to lose the whole body. See Matthew 5, 29-30.

I would like to add to this; it is better to lose you're mind than to lose your soul.

My goal is to get this letter circulating around the world and this in all possible languages. This is also the goal of Jesus and the will of God. See Matthew 28, 19-20; 'Therefore go and make disciples of all nations, and teaching them to obey everything I have commanded you, and surely I am with you always, to the very end of the age.'

Now if you want to be part of Jesus' gang you can make as many copies as you can of this letter and send them to as many people as you can. It is possible also to do everything you can to stop it and to get me executed. The decision is totally yours and so will be your judgement in front of Jesus (the word of God). Jesus said he will be with us until the end of the age and truly the word of God is still with us.

There is another very important message which is coming from God and this is the one that is in Isaiah 42, 1. 'Behold, my servant, whom I uphold, my chosen one in whom my soul delight. I have put my Spirit upon him; he will bring forth justice to the nations.'

Justice here really means freedom.

See also Matthew 12, 18. 'Behold, my servant whom I have chosen; my beloved in whom my soul is well-pleased; I will put my Spirit on him, and he shall proclaim justice to the nations.'

Now, if Jesus was really born God, would God have had to put his Spirit on him, so he can do everything God command him? God said Jesus was his servant and that He chose him, his beloved one. Do we really choose our biological children?

It is the work of Jesus I continue as one of his disciples.

See also Isaiah 7, 14, which is another proof that Jesus was born just like any other babies in the world and he had to learn like everyone else what is right and wrong and since he started his ministry at the age of thirty; he was under the laws of men as well. I will come back on this a bit farther though.

See Isaiah 7, 14-15. 'Therefore the Lord Himself will give you a sign: Behold, a virgin will be with child and bear a son and she will call his name Immanuel. He will eat curds and honey at the time he knows enough to refuse evil and choose good.'

Excuse me, but to me this is not the description of a child born God.

This is the truth either you believe in it or not. Jesus was chosen by God to tell us everything God commanded him; the good news that it was possible to be saved by the repentance, no matter what the sin is for as long we turn away from it and only God can give us the strength to do it. This can be impossible to men, but nothing is impossible to God, except doing wrong, of course.

God said that his servant, Jesus will save many, but this is to be done with the word of God. It is with the truth that Jesus saves and not with his death on the cross like the liar told you.

See Isaiah 53, 11. '<u>By his knowledge</u> my righteous one, my servant will save many.'

Now, for Jesus to begin his ministry at the age of thirty; there is an explanation for this too.

We have to know that to be a Rabbi a man has to be at least thirty, have at least ten followers and be married.

Now, if we are careful to what we read in the New Testament of the Bible we can count thirteen times where Jesus was called by his apostles Rabbi without having him to deny even once.

There is a very important message from Jesus in Matthew 24, 15. 'Therefore when you see the abomination of desolation which was spoken through by the prophet Daniel, standing in the holy place, (in the Bible) may the reader be careful when he reads.'

This is what I ask you too, to be careful, not only about what you read, but to whom you are talking to and mainly how you do it, because the beast is always ready to kill if it thinks it is necessary for its survival. Don't you ever forget what happened to Jesus and to Louis Riel. This really happened, these are not invented stories.

There is another sure thing; the beast already started the war against me. According to what it's written in revelation 11, there will be two prophets who will have the power to do great things. I don't believe everything which is written in Revelation for the simple reason that most of it was written by the John of Paul or by Paul himself. The author of Revelation is talking too much about the Paul's seven churches to be the Jesus' John, the apostle.

Do you see? If this was a lie, a person could wait a very long time to see someone change the water to blood like it is written in Revelation 11, 6.

This year the plagues are in big numbers in the world. I can't forget also that many of my enemies fell dead almost in my presence. There are a lot of big fires in British Columbia since they persecuted me unfairly. The province of Alberta too is burning a lot and is flooding almost continually. If they ever think I am responsible for these disasters they will have an extra reason to take my life.

From James Prince who invites you to spread the truth just like Jesus asked us to do by the will of God, the Father.

CHAPTER 6

The Word of God To Be Spread Out. The Truth The Jesus' Disciples Must Diffuse Around The World And The Lies They Must Unveil Like Louis Riel Did It.

It is very possible I repeat myself on many occasions and I make a number of mistakes in my writing, since I have a low level of education like the Jesus apostles and the cost of getting my work corrected is too high for my finances. I was told the price would be around $2000.00.

There are things we cannot repeat often enough and Jesus most of the time chose people with little education to follow him, but they were honest and courageous. Besides, if I repeat myself so often it is because Paul repeated his lies and contradictions a lot.

If you accepted Paul's repeated lies and contradictions, you must be able to accept my repeated true statements about the truth also.

It is even strange if I keep writing today in this book after the terrible night I just went through.

At supper time last night I put a fry pan on the stove with oil in it to make myself a good homemade French fries while my hamburger meat was cooking in another one. The potatoes I had on hand were just too big for my hunger; so I went to the basement the pick one up that was more appropriated.

I noticed at that point the water was rising rapidly and the water pump was probably defective. I then unplugged and plugged this pump many times, but there was no change to the problem. So I left in a hurry to go get another pump I unplugged lately at the hall which I also own. I didn't want to take the new pump over there for fear the hall might get flooded too. Then I rushed back to the house and I'm sure the whole thing didn't take more than ten minutes.

When I arrived at the house I noticed right away through the window that the oil left on the stove was in flame. I rushed out of my vehicle a bit excited and I went to the door that was locked and I realized the keys were still in the van. Of course I rushed again to my vehicle to grab the keys and then I opened the door from a house that was full of smoke. It was completely impossible to breathe in there.

The very worst was that my dog and my cat were in this house; so I went in there and I opened the two doors and all the windows I could. My rooster that lives in the basement even though it was well perched was very scared. I left the doors and windows opened for about fifteen minutes and because it was very windy the smoke was out quickly. Then I went to get this pump in my vehicle and I rushed to the basement to install it.

It is not this simple when we don't have everything we need to do it. The hose was too short to reach the only exit that is there; which is the dryer exit. Ho, there was another piece of hose, but their ends were the same size and neither one wanted to leave the other one enter. What to do then? There was nothing on hand that could help me join the two together. I had to think fast because the water kept rising pretty fast. Pretty soon my boots wouldn't be high enough and the water was very close to the freezing point. So I took a lighter that I use from time to time to light up the wood stove I got in the basement and I heated up one end of a hose which just made it smaller enough to enter the other one. The trick worked. I also had to find a string to hold the hose up which didn't want to stay in place because of the water pressure. I also had to find an extension cord to get this pump to function.

This is normally a very simple thing to do, but water and electricity are not two things that get along very well when they touch each other.

I looked up wondering what in the world I was going to do and there was the cord I needed right above my head. It is a cord that runs through the floor to feed my computer, the one I'm writing on now. I had to hold this pump with my hands a good hour before enough water was out fearing every minute an electric choc and allowed me to find another string to hold this pump in place. Three times these hoses got separated and forced me to unplug the pump each time. I also had to go down to the basement every ten minutes to kick this pump that didn't want to start or stop on its own from six in the afternoon until two o'clock in the night. This is why I had a flood in the hall as well a month earlier, which caused me to take out at least one ton of ice with five gallons pails. It was quite an exercise to climb the stairs up and down with two full pails of fifty pounds each of ice for two days.

Getting back to the house and the flood now; the pump was taking out about one hundred gallons of water every ten minutes or so. I then realized it was not because the pump wasn't working, but because it couldn't take out all the water that was coming in and at the time I didn't know how. At two o'clock in the morning when I was completely exhausted and sleepy like I never was I decided to bring this last pump back and exchange it for the new one I installed in the hall a month ago. This would allow me to go to sleep at four in the morning. This was quite a marathon, but a man has to do what he has to do.

April is the time of the year when there is a blanket of ice at a certain level in the ground and all the melted snow and ice, all these tons of water break through and the basement is the perfect place for it as a refuge.

I got up at around noon and even before taking my breakfast I started writing this story you're reading. Then I suddenly thought I better go check the pump at the hall. I didn't know if there was still a problem over there, but I decided to go quickly. Sure enough, this pump couldn't work without being kicked. I had to work another five hours there with a vacuum to take out about two thousand gallons of water.

I usually go to the basement every four or five hours to put wood in the stove to keep the house tempered. Because of a potato that was too big at the time I was saved from a sure disaster.

I got many things in the basement including electric tools, like a compressor and saws, drills and so on, but the worst would have been the water to reach the motor of the pump which is connected to the power. In four to five hours the water could have reach up to six feet high.

Just like Joseph was warned in a vision about the danger for the baby and the mother this potato was the instrument which allowed me to avoid some very costly damages.

A dream, a vision, a thought, an idea, don't neglect any of them, because they are tools God, the Father uses to inform us about our needs, the danger, the threats and mainly to take the best road for us. That we pay attention to his voice, to our thoughts, to our ideas, to our visions can be a question of life or death, so believe it, it is worth paying attention. Do this and good luck.

A stranger asked me: 'Who are you?' I told him; "I am a son of God, I am a God's disciple like Jesus, Moses and the others who listened to his voice." "How can you say such a thing?" "You're not going to try to crucify or to stone me if I tell you and I give you many information? Do you realize that I risk my life today for telling you these things that I know? But to tell you the truth; doing so brings me the most joy, to accomplish the will of God, my Father." "Isn't it written that Jesus is God only son?" "This is what is written in John 3, 16, but I will show you differently and this with something that is also written in the Bible, the book about the truth.

Look in Exodus 4, 22-23." "'Thus says the Lord, 'Israel is my son, <u>my firstborn</u>. So I said to you, 'Let my son go so he may serve Me.' ' "

"Now, would you say that God is a liar or a certain John is? I just know that the Jesus' John, the apostle wouldn't have lied. Take a look also in Luke 3, 38." "'Adam, the son of God.'"

"There is more yet in Deuteronomy 32, 18-19." "'You neglected the rock who begot you and forgot the God who gave you birth. The Lord saw this and spurned them because of the provocation of his <u>sons</u> and daughters.'

God has many children. I am his son too. Yes God has many children and He didn't need a woman to make Adam and neither a virgin to make Jesus. And if Jesus is not from the seed of Joseph, he simply can't be the Messiah, which means the Christ like it was announced by God's prophets or else all his prophets are liars too, which is impossible.

Here is one thing Jesus said to the ones who listened to him, the one who followed him. The will of God is that we listen to his servant, Jesus, the one He sent us. See Matthew 17, 5. 'While he was still speaking, a bright cloud overshadowed them, and behold, a voice out of the cloud said. 'This is my son, with whom I am well-pleased; listen to him.' '

There is one thing to notice here. God said; 'My son.' He didn't say my only son. Now, this is the same Jesus, God's son who said; see Matthew 12, 50. 'For whoever does the will of my Father who is in heaven, he is my brother and sister and mother.'

This means that if you can count all the ones who do the will of the Father in heaven and all those who did then you can count all of God's children, but don't waste your time; God knows them all already and He knows me. God is the God of all of the living; meaning all the ones who live their life off sin, all the ones who have sincerely repented and turned away from their sin. This is what Jesus told us and this is far away from an only begotten son. If you don't believe me believe in Jesus and in God, then you'll get the truth." "I have to give you this." "The ones who say that Jesus is God make me God's brother." "Are you out of your mind?" "You don't think this makes sense?" "God' brother, I would have heard it all from you."

"Don't you know how to read and how to understand? They say that Jesus is God and the same Jesus said, not me, but Jesus said that whoever does the will of his Father in heaven, which I do, is his brother. So I am God' brother according to Christianity.

I personally say that God is my Father that evidently Jesus is the son of God too, but not the only one and I am Jesus' brother because I too do the will of my Father who is in heaven. Listen, it's not me who said Jesus is God.

Now, if we believe the words of the more ancient God's prophets to whom God revealed Himself we will understand that Jesus just like the other prophets had his own tribulations of human beings like Moses and King David, who both have killed a human being and this didn't stop God from using both of them to his service.

Take a good look in Isaiah 7, 14-15." "'Therefore the Lord Himself will give you a sign: Behold, a virgin will be with child and bear a son and she will call his name Immanuel. He will eat curds and honey at the time he knows enough to refuse evil and choose good.'"

"This to me is not the description of God made man by the operation of the Holy Spirit who was not yet in the world according to John 14, 26, because Jesus was not yet glorified.

See John 14, 26. 'But the Helper, the Holy Spirit, whom the Father will sent in my name, he will teach you all things, and bring to your remembrance all that I said to you.'

See also John 14, 16, 15, 26, 16, 7, 16, 13 and Acts 2, 4. Note too that there is no reference to this at all in Matthew. There would be a lot to write on this subject; I'd say a whole chapter. I will though add another point. See John 7, 39. 'But this he spoke of the Spirit, whom those who believed in him were to receive; for <u>the Spirit was not yet given</u>, because Jesus was not yet glorified.'

But see what is written in Matthew 1, 18. Mary was with child by the Holy Spirit of Jesus who was not yet glorified for sure.

According to another author Jesus would have died on Friday afternoon and resurrected on Sunday morning and this contradicts Jesus himself. See Matthew 12, 40. 'For just like Jonah was <u>three days and three nights</u> in the belly of a sea monster, so will be the Son of Man be three days and three nights in the heart of the earth.'

They just have eliminated one night and one and a half day because the employers just knew it was cheaper to give money to the church to lie than to pay for another day off to the employees.

The ones who say Jesus is God are mostly Christians, but it is not really their fault; they have received such a brain washing, they were blinded so much by the lies that it is hard for them now to receive the truth. This will take a miracle, which can only happen with the word of God, the truth. This is the real reason of our discussion." "Do you mean they won't believe you?" "It is very hard for them to receive the true when they believed the lies for so long.

Although it is their own fault, their own guilt if they continue to believe in the lies when they took notice of the truth."

"You were asking me if I would crucify or stone you if you were telling me the truth. If you are the son of God like Jesus and Moses you shouldn't be afraid to die." "Why are you telling me this? They both suffered a lot and they are both dead. I'm not afraid to die or of anything else, but I'm not stupid enough to ignore the danger, the threat that is above my head. If they have killed the Master, Jesus, I'm sure they will think about killing a member of his family. Besides, Jesus told us so. Take a look in Matthew 10 from verse 7 to 42. See Matthew 10, 7-8. 'As you go preach this message: 'The kingdom of heaven is near. Heal the sick, raise the dead, cleanse those who have leprosy, drive out demons. Freely you have received, freely give. Do not take along any gold or silver or copper in your belts; take no bag for the journey, or extra tunic, or sandals or a staff; for the worker is worth his keep.' '

How many of the church's leaders did you hear say: 'Keep your money'? How many of them did you hear preach: 'Don't call anyone on earth; 'Father, Rabbi, pastor, director'? Or worst yet; 'Holy father'?

I heal the sick, I chase demons and I raise the dead and this doesn't cost anyone money. I received freely and I give freely. I never met a person with leprosy yet, but I'm sure I could heal him with peroxide like I did too with the polyps that were in my nose. They disappeared and if I could go any farther in my sinuses I wouldn't have needed a surgery like the specialist told me." "I would like to see you heal the sick and raise the dead from my own eyes." "Don't you see that you are healing right now and pretty soon you will be resurrected from the dead? When Jesus was sitting and talking with the sinners, the publicans, what did he say to them?" "I don't really know." "He didn't say: 'I don't really know.' But he said what you can read in Matthew 9, 12. 'On hearing this Jesus said; 'It is not the healthy (the sinless people) who need a doctor, (the word of God) but the sick.' (The sinners).

Let me translate this in your language for you. It is not the ones who live their live off sin who need the Saviour the most, the word of God, but the sinners. If you live with the mortal sin, you are dead and if you cleanse yourself by repenting and turn away from your sin, then you are resurrected." "Now I start to understand. With the word of God and only with it you can bring me towards God." "This is what Jesus said and you can read it in John 14, 6. 'Jesus answered; 'I am the way and the truth and the life, no one comes to the Father except through me.'

If I translate this again, we get; 'No one comes to the Father except through the word of God.'

This includes the word of God that was put in the mouth of all the other God's prophets before Jesus and after Jesus also." "So this means that I will be healed of my slavery of sin and then I will be resurrected from the dead. I go from the family of the devil and enter the family of God, the family of the living, because God is the God of the living. This is what Jesus was doing." "Hay, you progress rapidly. I can say those things because

I listen to Jesus, to the word of God and to the other prophets who were there before him. I listen to his voice also when He talks to me through my dreams and my visions either Himself or with his angels. He speaks to me also through thoughts and divine ideas like the ones to write this book and hymns and songs that are out of the ordinary and please God.

See Numbers 12, 6-8. 'He said; "Listen to my words: When a prophet of the Lord is among you, I reveal Myself to him in visions, I speak to him in dreams, but this is not true with my servant Moses; he is faithful in all my house. With him I speak face to face, cleanly and not in riddles; he sees the form of the Lord. Why then were you not afraid to speak against my servant Moses.' "

Paul did it; I mean spoke against Moses.

God said He was talking face to face with Moses and He also said that his servant He will rise up from the brothers in Israel will be like Moses. This is the reason why I know Jesus received his commands directly from God and I listen to Jesus." "What are you doing beside all this?" "My answer might be chocking to you. First I have to tell you that in French, I am and I follow translate the same way. I am (I follow) the God of Israel, the One who has created everything and forgives the sins of everyone who repented and turned to God. I am (I follow) Jesus of Nazareth, the one they crucified because he was telling the truth. Like him I heal the sick and I resurrect the dead. I am (I follow) the word of God in everything it says; the word of God that makes miracles. All these things happen with the word of God." "Can I be healed and saved if I touch you?" "You'll touch me and you will be saved the day you will live by the word of God, the day you'll follow God's Law and his commandments and you'll touch me even more the day you will spread out the word of God, the truth. I will know then that I touched you or God touched you through the teaching I brought to you." "Don't you think you are pushing a bit much when you say; 'I am the God of Israel, I am Jesus of Nazareth?" "OK, let me translate this again for you. I told you that I am and I follow translate the same way in French. So, what I said is; I follow the God of Israel and I follow Jesus of Nazareth. I don't see what is wrong with this. I only tell the truth. If you look in Thessalonians 2, 1-17, you will see that it is the ones who believe the truth who are saved." "This was written by Paul, isn't it?" "This is what they want you to believe, but I don't believe Paul was the author of those lines. I will explain this to you another time if you don't mind." "I'm intrigued." "I will tell you only this for now which is a message from Jesus written in Matthew 7, 18. 'A good tree cannot bear bad fruit and a bad tree cannot bear good fruit.'

This means we will recognize the liar by his lies and the one who tells the truth with the truth and the two of them can be verified." "Tell me then, how can we tell it is the truth?" "Contrary to what this seems to be; it is very easy to see the truth between the two of them." "Not for me." "It will be for you too if you listen carefully." "This is what you think." "You'll see. Although you have to keep your eyes opened, have an open mind and want to know the truth. You see, the ones who are telling the truth like Jesus and Moses lead you towards God, the Father, Creator of the earth and heaven and not towards a certain religion or a certain church." "So, you are against religions?" "Just like Jesus is." "What are you telling me now?" "The truth and this according to Jesus. Go read in Matthew 23, from 8-10 where Jesus tells his apostles not to let themselves be called Rabbi and not to call anyone on earth father or religious director.

Don't you forget also that pastor means just the same thing." "Wow, the religions are taking a big punch with this one." "This is the exact reason why I was telling you I was risking my life by talking to you with my knowledge about these things. Why do you think they were looking for Jesus and tried to catch him with the thought of killing him?" "Because the religions of the time were affected." "At least this is something you understood.

According to John 3, 16. 'For God so loved the world that He gave his one and only son, that whoever believes in him shall not perish but have eternal life.'

To me and to Isaiah 66, 3, this verse is a terrible abomination in the holy place, in the Bible, just like Jesus mentioned it in Matthew 24, 15. 'So when you see standing in the holy place the abomination that causes desolation spoken of through the prophet Daniel—let the reader understand.'

In the French Bible, the last four word of this verse tell differently. It is written; 'May the reader be careful when he reads.

So, this is it. I paid attention and this is why I found Isaiah 66, 3. Now pay attention to what it is written in there. Isaiah 66, 3. 'But whoever sacrifices a bull is like one who kills a man, and whoever offers a lamb, (like they say God did) is like the one who breaks a dog's neck; whoever makes a grain offering is like one who presents pig's blood and whoever burns memorial incense, is like one who worships an idol. They have chosen their own ways and their souls delight in their <u>abominations</u>.'

I said it before I found Isaiah 66, 3 that it was an abomination to say God sacrificed his one and only son. As far as I know the priests in the Catholic Church are still burning incense in their services on the first day of the week. Now, this too according to Isaiah is another abomination; even though I don't think it is the worst. But the worst of all is in John 3, 16. You have most likely heard this one from John 1, 29: 'The next day John saw Jesus coming toward him and said; 'Look, the Lamb of God, (an animal) who takes away the sin of the world.'

If John the Baptist said this it was enough to be beheaded, but I don't believe he did. This is another lie, another venom, another abomination the John of Paul put in the holy place, in the Bible.

It wasn't enough for God's enemies to say the son of God, the one God chose to tell us the truth, his word, is an animal, they went as far as saying God sacrificed his son, this animal to save the sinners, as if this has a price.

It is also written somewhere else that this is an abomination. See 2 Kings 16, 3. 'He walked in the ways of the kings of Israel and even sacrificed his son in the fire following the detestable ways of the nations the Lord had driven out before the Israelites.'

Now, the Lord would have driven out these abominations before the Israelites and He would have Himself done the same thing with his son Jesus????????? Please.........

This is enough desolation done to me to make me sick to my stomach. It is evil, demon possess people who killed Jesus and other prophets, not God. God allowed men like Jesus to sacrifice themselves because He wants us to know the truth, his justice, the least we can do is to believe it.

God so loved the world that if it wasn't for Noah, He would have destroyed it all, because of their sins. The kingdom of Jesus, the kingdom of heaven is not of this world, because he is the king of the just and not the king of the sinners, just like God is not the god of the sinners, the god of the dead. God and Jesus want to save the sinners from the devil's trap, from this slavery of sin. Do you see, the truth is not welcome in this world today more than it was at the time of Jesus? See, Jesus is the King of the kingdom of heaven, which is separated from the rest of the world, but which is still on earth. See what is written in Matthew 27, 11. 'Are you the king of the Jews?' 'Yes, it is as you say.' Jesus replied.'

From which world are the Jews?" "From our world." "Now, go read John 18, 36." "'Jesus said; 'My kingdom is not of this world.'"

"Only Matthew reported Jesus' messages talking about the Kingdom of heaven, including the one where Jesus gave the keys to his kingdom to Peter, the most considerate of his apostles. See Matthew 16, 19. 'I will give you the keys of the kingdom of heaven; what ever you bind on earth will be bound in heaven, and whatever you loose on earth will be loosed in heaven.'

This is the greatest power Jesus gave to his disciples and I know it is a power I have. Jesus knew he was going to die soon and this is why he acted like this. Jesus didn't need to be a scientist to know how much many people wanted him dead and he also knew it was just a matter of time before this happens. Do you see now that these keys made it up to me and in turn I can open the doors of the kingdom of heaven to others and it is with the truth and with the truth only that I can do it? I can only do it with the Jesus' messages. Only the truth, the word of God can open the doors of the kingdom of heaven and none can enter it unless he repented for his sins and become as pure, as innocent as doves, as innocent as young children.

CHAPTER 7

The three billions and a half Christians, the Moslems and the communists don't want to hear about the word of God, about the truth and neither do the supposedly J…..Witnesses." "But why are you saying such a thing? You have at least seven billions enemies by saying this." "I told you I was risking my life by talking to you about the word of God. Don't you think they are enough out there to kill me? And you can be sure of one thing, Jesus had one trader out of twelve and I will get one faithful out of twelve." "Then you too want to create a religion?" "Not more than Jesus wanted too. I want to lead you and others to God. You and everyone to whom I will talk to and just like Jesus; I don't want any money from you or from anyone else. I want to form disciples who will do what I do, meaning, spreading the Jesus' messages, the word of God and unveil the liars and their lies to the world. This is what Jesus asked his disciples to do and you can read it in Matthew 28, 19-20.

Do you know a religion like this one?" "I have to admit it, I don't." "If my books ever bring me some money it will be money earned honestly and most of it will be used to translate them in every possible language with the goal to alert all the nations, the entire world.

All the religions where the Bible is use the way I know it with all the messages of Paul inside the New Testament and the ones who preach Paul instead of Jesus are antichrist and this with no doubt at all in my mind. I heard many times and this from many different people that the Koran was almost identical to the Bible; which means that Paul is in there too.

If Jesus wanted to form the kind of religions or the kind of churches that we know he had the power to do it since he was a carpenter and he had the four and five thousands men who was following him. But contrary to the leaders of nowadays Jesus was teaching them and sent them on their way. When he started his ministry he left all of his tools behind him and according to the scriptures he was not carrying any money and he had no place to rest his head.

At the time of Jesus it was not rare a man was walking with bare feet or in sandals, but today if I would try to reach people on foot on the highways I would not have enough time with one hundred lives to alert all the nations. Gas is not very cheap either. So God gave me or showed me a different way, which is a bit more appropriated for our time to reach all the nations and there is nothing like the writing to do it. The words die but the writing stays.

According to my calculations there are only like twenty years or so before the final world wide conflict; I mean the Armageddon war, if this is the name of the last world war. Everything is already in place. The religions war is already started between the Christians, the Moslems and the communists." "So, you'll have to move quickly." "You said it." "How will you do it?" "God showed me the way to reach all of the nations in a very short time. He also gave me what it takes to become the richest man of my country in less than five years and the richest man in the world in less than ten years." "Wow, this is like a miracle." "You said it." "This will be just as historical as the tower of Babel." "Can you tell me what this is all about?" "No, but you will hear about it very soon." "Well, all I can say is you are quite intriguing and mysterious." "All the money or almost will be used to make the truth known around the world contrary to what the religions have done. I will begin by buying television stations just about everywhere. Then I will produce movies like we have never seen before, which will talk like I do with you. You can imagine the rest. I am a carpenter just like Jesus and his father Joseph was and I can't wait to leave my tools behind like Jesus did." "Would you do like Jesus and leave everything behind like he did?" "Do you know many people today who would feed me for listening to the things they don't want to hear? I would certainly die from starvation." "I have to admit that you are facing an enormous enemy." "Even some members of my own family don't want to hear what I have to say and they are ready to send me out of their house for the things I say and yet, all I do is repeating the messages of Jesus to people who pretend loving God. But this too Jesus predicted it. You can read it in Matthew 10, 36. 'A man's enemies will be the members of his own household.'

Jesus was sure right about this one too." "Will you have a few friends?" "I sure hope you will be one of them. Up until now you seem to want to listen and to learn a bit more each time. What you will do with all this information only God knows. I only know that Jesus gave me the only possible recipe to become one of his disciples, to discover the kingdom of heaven and to get eternal life." "What is this recipe you're talking about so often?" "You can find it in Matthew 22, 35-40. 'One of them, an expert in the law, tested Jesus with this question: 'Teacher, which is the greatest commandment in the Law?' Jesus replied; 'Love the Lord your God with all your heart and with all your soul and with all you mind. This is the greatest commandment. And the second one is like it; love your neighbour as yourself. All the Law and the Prophets hang on these two commandments.' '

This, my friend is the recipe Jesus gave us to receive eternal life. When we love God with all our heart we love his Law too. You might have noticed too there is one story and two versions about this one. The story in Luke is different from the one in Matthew. See Luke 10, 25-28. 'On one occasion an expert in the law stood up to test Jesus. 'Teacher,' he asked, 'What must I do to inherit eternal life?' 'What is written in the Law?' Jesus replied. 'How do you read it?' He answered; 'Love the Lord your God with all of you heart and with all of your soul and with all of your strength and with all your mind and love your neighbour as yourself.' 'You have answered correctly.' Jesus replied, 'Do this and you will live.' '

Now here if you noticed, it is not Jesus who tells the other what to do to get eternal life, but an expert in the Law does. In Matthew it is Jesus who told the other what is the greatest commandment in the Law and what to do the get eternal life. One is lying and this is not Matthew. Jesus didn't say these two commandments were replacing the whole Law, but on these two commandments hang the Law and the prophets; which is a huge difference. Each time Jesus said; 'Come to me.' Or when he said; 'The one who listen to me.' He doesn't speak about him as a man, but about the word of God. A very nice example is this one; 'No one comes to the Father but through me.'

Which means; 'No one comes to the Father but through the word of God.'

See again Deuteronomy 18, 18.

Jesus, the word of God. See Matthew 19, 14. 'Jesus said; 'Let the little children come to me, and do not hinder them, for the kingdom of heaven belongs to such as these.'

Again this means; 'Let the little children come to the word of God.'

I heard a priest on a radio talk show in Quebec City one time saying this would be scandalous to hear any man saying something like this today. See, to him this was like paedophilia, which he most likely was, the priest I mean.

Take a look in Matthew 6, 5-6.

See, Jesus told us who to pray, how to pray and when to pray. Jesus went even farther than this; he told us what to say when we pray. He told us not to be like the hypocrites who pray on the street corners like the J….Witnesses do or before the assemblies like Christians do, the priests, the pastors, many church leaders, so they can be noticed by others. Who are they following? Not Jesus. They are following Paul who said to pray everywhere, but Jesus the true Messiah told us to pray in our room, which means in private. If you follow the antichrist, you are antichrist too. Do you recognize many of them? A Jesus' disciples will never tell you to pray other idols like the Virgin Mary, who was not a virgin anymore when she died or all the saints that are not, because Jesus said that only One is good and he wasn't even talking about himself, but about the Father who is in heaven.

Jesus told us to go in our room to pray, to pray the Father and that only He could grant us our wish. Jesus was pulling himself away from others to pray and most of the time he went on top of a mountain to do it. He had no room to go to, no place to rest his head.

But again with this one Paul said the exact opposite, but just like the devil in the Garden of Eden it looked like it was the right thing to say, it looked like it was the truth. See 1 Timothy 2, 8. 'I want men to lift holy hands in prayers everywhere without anger and disputing.'

If they listen to Jesus and pray in their room there would be no reason for disputes.

Jesus, the Christ told us not to be babbling vain prayers like the pagans do and still doing and who are they praying? Mary, Joseph, Jesus and all the imaginable saints, idols. See the first God's commandment in Exodus 20, 3. 'You shall have no other god before Me.' "

"Why did you say: 'The J….Witnesses? You don't pronounce the name of God?" "Do you remember I told you that I follow Jesus?" "I remember very well, yes." "Then find a place where Jesus pronounced the name of his Father who is in heaven out of the Bible of these J….Witnesses of course. Do you know the second God's commandment which is written in Exodus 20, 7?" "Vaguely, I must admit it." "Take the Bible and read." "'You shall not misuse the name of the Lord your God, for the Lord will not hold guiltless who misuses his name.' "

Misuse means in vain, unnecessary, isn't it?" "This is pretty well it, yes." "Do I have to pronounce the name of God for you to understand who I was talking about?" "I have to admit it again; I understood without having you to pronounce his name alright." "These so called Witnesses are taking the name of the

Lord unnecessarily in the face of the world and by doing this they make people doing the same thing either they talk about them for the good or for the bad in 99% of the time. If they had respect for the name of Lord and his Law like Jesus has and like I do now; they would change their name in a hurry." "I never thought about this before, but now that you are talking about it I understand that you are right and I just learned another very good message." "In every hold Bible I read I only saw the name of the Lord in one book only and this was in Psalm 83, 18. Now, if you read this Psalm completely you will see that this author has a totally different policy than Jesus about forgiving and a totally different way to ask God the way He should threat his enemies. If the Witnesses have chosen this one to build their religion on there is no wonder they are so antichrist. I am glad to see that in most of the Bibles I worked with the authors have respected the second God's commandment and they have replaced the name of the Lord in this Psalm with God's title. Bravo!

No one can hide behind God's face and no where else for this matter. God can see everything and everybody and if He can count all of my hairs, He can also count all the ones who disobey Him as well.

All the novenas, the rosaries, the ways of the cross are some obvious examples of babbling prayers in vain and at the same time it is idolatry. Don't you complain to God if your dead idols don't make your wish come through, because God turns his face the other way from these impious." "You said Jesus told us when to pray." "Yes, this is when you pray, when you want to. Jesus told us that only One is good. He wasn't talking about himself, but about his Father who is in heaven. See Matthew 19, 16-17. 'Now a man came up to Jesus and asked, 'Teacher, what good thing I must do to get eternal life?' 'Why do you ask me about what is good?' Jesus replied. 'There is only One who is good. If you want to enter life, obey the commandments.' ' The Law.

You will understand that Paul said the exact opposite, that we are no longer under the supervision of the Law, but that we are under the grace.

You can pray an individual to help you for as long as he is alive, but when he is dead, what can he do for you? The very last words from Jesus are written in Matthew 28, 20. 'And surely I am with you always, to the very end of the age.'

Don't you forget one thing; Jesus was talking to the ones who followed him, the ones who listen to him, meaning his apostles, his disciples. It is still true today. Before all this Jesus said; 'I am the light, I am the way, the life, the truth.' This is the exact description of the word of God.

I too follow the light, I too follow his voice, I too follow the word of God which takes me to God. Not to forget also the word of God to Moses, which is written in Deuteronomy 18, 18-19. 'I will raise up for them a prophet like you (Moses, who is not God) from among their brothers; I will put my words in his mouth, and he will tell them everything I command him. If anyone does not listen (and they are many) to my words that the prophet speaks in my name, I myself will call him to account.'

Now you are warned by God Himself and you will not have valid excuses before him at the last judgement if you didn't repent. I don't sin no more." "How can this be possible and how can you say this?" "It is not by my own will that I can do it, but by the will of God that this can be accomplished. It is most likely because Jesus was living his life off sin they said he was God, because sinners can't conceive it is possible for a human being. It is true that it is impossible for a human being's will alone and Jesus mentioned it before me. See Matthew 19, 25-26. 'When the disciples heard this, they were greatly astonished and asked, 'Who then can be saved?' Jesus looked at them and said; 'With man this is impossible, but with God all things are possible.' '

This is why I can live my life without sin, because God is with me." "But are we not all saved by the blood of Jesus on the cross, us all who believe in him?" "This is what the liars want you to believe, but this is not what the word of God put in Jesus' mouth said." "Oh boy, you are changing all the facts now." "It's not me who is changing the facts, but the facts have been changed by the liars." "Explain to me then, because I'm losing you." "Of course I will explain this to you. Do you believe in the word of God that was put in Jesus' mouth?" "I sure would like to." "Then listen carefully to this because it is the key of the whole humanity. This is the teaching of Jesus. Look in Matthew 13, 41. 'The Son of Man (Jesus) will send out his angels, and they will weed out of his kingdom everything that causes sin and all who do evil.'

Do you see now that it is the ones who listen to Jesus who are saved and not the ones who believe in him and continue to sin?

You know too that the devil and his demons also believe in Jesus and in God and this maybe more than anyone else and shudder, because they know their destiny and they also know the power of God. Look also in Matthew 25, 41. 'Depart from me you evil doer into the eternal fire prepared for the devil and his angels.'

Do you see that in the kingdom of God there will be no more scandals and neither anyone who commits sins? On the other hand the kingdom of heaven is besieged. See Matthew 11, 12. 'From the days of John the Baptist until now, the kingdom of heaven has been forcefully advancing, and forceful men lay hold of it.'

To understand better who are the devil and his angels we have to go back to Matthew 13, 36 and read carefully the explanation of the parable of the weeds. You see, Jesus came to teach us the truth, the good seed, but Jesus' enemy, the devil showed up at the same time to sow the weeds, the lies and this is still happening today if we are not careful to what we read, to what ever is in the scriptures. This is why Jesus warned us in Matthew 24, 15. 'May the reader be careful when he reads.'

There is a very important reason why Jesus gave us this warning and this is because the devil's trap is right there in the scriptures, in the Bible. A member of my family told me one day: 'The Bible, you have to take it all or not at all.'

There you are; the reason why I found all those lies and contradictions is exactly because I took it all or almost, I find Numbers very boring.

Thanks to my brother-in-law; without knowing it he made a very nice deed to God and to the humanity.

But we have to give credit where credit is due. Paul has created the largest religious empire in the world. This empire is rich and it is powerful. There are one point two billions Catholics in the world. Just put them at one hundred dollars each and they could finance another world war again. This is not counting that many people within this billion who could put a lot more than one hundred. This is the Catholic Church alone and what about the whole Christianity? What is it? Three and a half billions. This is quite a beast!

At the time gold was worth $39.00 an ounce, a man came on television and said the chalice was worth sixty thousands dollars and the ciborium was worth one hundred thousands dollars in gold. Today gold is worth thirty-eight times more and this is according to the Stock Market. This means that according to a little calculation the chalice today is worth two million two hundred and eighty thousand dollars and the ciborium is worth close to four millions dollars.

These are many dollars that would never return to the pockets of those blind donors. It is not surprising some of their properties were given away for a dollar like I noticed in Grand-Mère Quebec and they are keeping their nice and big heavy doors locked in the buildings they keep.

This huge empire could simply not have been built without the help of the word of God though. Jesus knew it when he said: See Matthew 5, 18 and Matthew 24, 35. 'Heaven and earth will pass away, but my words will never pass away.'

This is why I say the antichrist used the word of God and falsified Jesus' messages and he mixed his letters with the Jesus' apostles' letters and all of this was to invent or to create Christianity.

You have to understand here that I don't say anything without having some proofs and all of them are coming from the Bible, the book about the truth.

See revelation 13, 18. 'This calls for wisdom. If anyone has insight, let him calculate the number of the beast, for it is man's number. His number is 666.'

Knowing that each letter has a number and they are worth 6 gradually; I found this name that I will reveal in time.

Here is how they read:

A = 6
B = 12
C = 18
D = 24 and so on until the end.

The word Catholic in French for example makes the number and so does computer, but the name of the beast is hidden better than this yet.

Since the one who wrote the verse 13, 18 of Revelation who I think was the devil himself in person and he challenged anyone to be smart enough to discover his number; thinking most likely it cannot be done by a human being. He has just been served, even though I am not at his service.

C,   18
A,   6
T, 120
H,   48
O,   90
L,   72
I,   54
Q, 102
U, 126
E,   30
Tot.666.

The one who has hidden the name of the beast, the creator of this beast who challenged the world to unveil his identity for the last two thousands years is the founder of this devilish empire. When one of his demons will read these lines I just wrote my life will be held by one hair. Although I know that nothing will happen to me that God, the Father wouldn't allow. Jesus said it in Matthew; 'And even the very hairs of your head are numbered.'

I lost a lot of them; this is why I know God spent time above my head.

Some said in the pass that the church is gone to hell. This is because he didn't know the church was hell or at least a very important tool of the devil.

Then Jesus said the wheat and the weeds will be together until the end of the world. See Matthew 13, 25-30.

Do you see that there is where we are today? The truth is getting separated from the lies and this is a job God gave me to do." "Where and when this all started for you?" "The day I asked God what I could do for Him instead of what He could do for me. So He took me to my word and since then I write, I invent, I compose and I sing praises to my God. It is absolutely wonderful. Here is one of my favourite Hymns I made for Him and it's called:

Praises To My Lord

I want to sing praises to my Lord with the angels,
With the angels of heaven.
And I want to be happy up there with the angels
And Adam, Eve and Abel.
I want to sing praises to my Lord with the angels,
With the angels of heaven
And I want to be happy up there with the angels
And with all of his children.
1 and 6
Listening to Jesus, to Jesus and Moses, this is how I have known the Father as my own
And because they told me, this is why I can see.
Yes now I can see through and I believe the truth.

2
I'll be able to meet the great Job and Jacob
Shake hands with Abraham, I am one of his fans.
I don't need Cadillac to meet with Isaac.
I'll sing with the angels, Daniel and Ezekiel.
3
I will seal with Noah and walk with Jeremiah
I'll fish with Hosea also with Isaiah.
I will build some mentions with David and Samson.
Be with the apostles and Jesus' disciples.
4
My heart is with Joseph who in prison was kept.
Was like me a dreamer didn't want to be sinner.
So my God was with him, kept him away from sin.
I'll meet him when ever there at the Lord's supper.
5
Now's the great gathering, will you be there to sing
With all of us one day in the heavens to pray?
The Lord is powerful; He's with whom is faithful.
He will not let you down, come join us in the round.
6
Listening to Jesus, to Jesus and Moses,
this is how I have known the Father as my own
And because they told me, this is why I can see.
Yes now I can see through and I believe the truth.

I want to sing praises to my Lord with the angels,
With the angels of heaven.
And I want to be happy up there with the angels
And Adam, Eve and Abel.
I want to sing praises to my Lord with the angels,
With the angels of heaven
And I want to be happy up there with the angels
And with all of his children.

Thank You my Lord for having delivered me from evil. Thank You my Lord for having opened my eyes. Thank You my Lord, thank You my Lord, thank You my Lord."

"Didn't Jesus say in this parable of the weeds he will send his angels to separate the lies from the truth?" "Go read it again, if you don't mind and be careful when you read, would you? Jesus said he will send his angels who will weed out of his kingdom everything that causes sin and all who do evil, meaning the ones who sin. The angels will separate the good people from the bad. I don't separate people at all, but I do some gardening. I separate the lies from the truth and this is the work of a Jesus' disciple. There is a big difference from the two assignments." "I admit it and I'm sorry." "No problem. There are many ignorant people who accused me of thinking myself as an angel; although I think that sometime I am guide by an angel." "You must believe in angels since you are talking about them this way?" "Jesus talked about them before me and I believe in him. Here are a few examples. See Matthew 13, 41. 'The Son of Man will send out his <u>angels</u> and they will weed out of his kingdom everything that causes sin and <u>all who do evil</u>. They will throw them into the fiery furnace, where there will be weeping and gnashing of teeth. Then the righteous will shine like the sun in the kingdom of their Father. He who has ears, let him hear."

See and it is very important Jesus in Matthew 16, 27. 'For the Son of Man is going to come in his Father's glory with <u>his angels</u> and then he will reward each person according to <u>what he has done</u>.'

Now, this is according to what one has done is not to what one <u>believes</u>, like Paul said.

See also Matthew 18, 10-12. 'See that you do not look down on one of these little ones. For I tell you that <u>their angels</u> in heaven always see the face of my Father in heaven.'

See also 2 Peter 2, 11. 'Yet even angels, although they are stronger and more powerful, do not bring slanderous accusations against such beings (demons) in the presence of the Lord.'

See Matthew 22, 30. 'At the resurrection people will neither marry nor be given in marriage; they will be like angels in heaven.' They will be faithful.

See also Matthew 26, 52-53. 'Put your sword back in its place.' Jesus said to him, 'For all who draw the sword will die by the sword. Do you think I cannot call on my Father and He will at once put at my disposal more than <u>twelve legions of angels</u>.'

See Matthew 13, 49. 'The angels will come and separate the wicked from the righteous.' Just as I said before.

See Matthew 13, 37-39. 'Jesus answered, 'The one who sowed the seed (the truth) is the Son of Man. (Jesus) The field is the world and the good seed stands for the sons of the kingdom. (The apostles, Jesus' disciples) The weeds are the sons of the evil one, (the demons, the wicked one) and the enemy who <u>sows</u> (present time) them is the devil. The harvest is the end of the age and the harvesters are <u>angels</u>.' '

See also Matthew 4, 11. 'Then the devil left him, and <u>angels</u> came and attended him.'

There must be some more, but these must be enough to convince you." "You're right; Jesus talked a lot about angels.

The Jesus' main goal, his most important message since he began his ministry is to pull us away from the slavery of sin. We can only be free if we listen to this message and execute his will. When Jesus began his ministry his first words when he started teaching were these ones in Matthew 4, 17. 'Repent for the kingdom of heaven is near.'

The kingdom of heaven is in the word of God Jesus brought to the world, so yes; it was very close to Jesus when he walked in to say; 'Repent.' This is when we go from death to life, from sinner to cleanse. How do you feel after a good shower? How do we feel after having done a good deed?

I made a kind of comparison between God towards men and a man, a master towards his dog. See the master is the master, but he is the one who feeds the animal, he is the one who gives the animal a shelter, who protects the animal the best he can, he is the one who picks up the poop on the ground, he is the one who cleans and brushes the animal in many cases and he is the one who trains, exercises and walks and all of this by spending as much time as possible with his best friend. In return the master asks the dog for obedience. The crazy dog who doesn't listen to his master has a very little chance to end his life with his master happy company. My dogs never take their food without thanking me in their own way. I love them a lot and they are sure returning this love back to me. It was the same with two pigs I kept in the pass. God created men, but I didn't create my animals. I only take care of them and yet my dogs, my cats and even my rooster adore me and are always looking for my hand that is always friendly with them." "There is a lot to think about in what you've just said." "Yes, it is very sad to say, but I believe there are more animals who adore their master than people who adore the true God.

When Jesus says: 'Go and live your life off sin, be perfect as your heavenly Father is perfect and observe the commandments.' He doesn't ask for the impossible. He's not a fool as many of them said he was.

Although many people are too blind to understand this." "Isn't it a sin to offend people?" "If this was the case, Jesus and even God would be sinners, because they both offended everyone who doesn't want to believe the truth." "But you have an answer for everything." "This is what they say being enlighten by the Holy Spirit. We know the truth and we cannot be fool by the liar anymore. This is frustrating the enemy to the point they want to kill us like this was the case for Jesus and Louis Riel. The enemy killed the body of Jesus, but he couldn't kill his soul, his spirit, the truth which lives forever. This is the eternal life.

For as long as my books don't make any differences for the finances of the churches, this will not be too dangerous for the Jesus' disciples." "What is it to be a disciple?" "The day you'll know, the day you'll be one you won't be asking questions anymore, but you'll do what I do; you will answer people questions to the ones who are looking for the truth. Be careful though, because just like this happened to Jesus, there will always be some of them to try to trap you. You wouldn't be thirsty for the truth anymore, because the truth will be in you and with you. Then you too will spread out the word of God." "Is this mean I have to leave everything?" "Peter had his wife, his house and also his mother-in-law and yet he was the most considerate of all the apostles and the one Jesus chose to carry the keys of the kingdom of heaven. His work changed from fishing fish to catch men to work for God. This is to show men the kingdom of heaven and what to do to enter it. Men have to get out of the slavery of sin. At times I think men like to be slaves. It is either sin, smoke, liquor, excess of food, games, drugs, work, sex, religion and more." "Aren't we all slaves of something?" "Not me, I am delivered from evil and I often thank God for it. The word of God has reached me and I make it fructify as much as I can. This is what Jesus called the good seed in the good soil. Many people are looking for it and don't find it, but when they will; they too will understand just like Matthew did that this is the most precious pearl, the kingdom of heaven, the fish cleanse from its guts. Matthew left everything to follow Jesus and yet all he had to do to make a good living was to sit and collect money. This soil will be fruitful and bring fruits to all the nations then the end will come.

The end of the actual world will be the end of the devil reign on people and the beginning of God's kingdom in which I will be. There is nothing any better than this. I have tears of joy every time I think about it while the wicked are trembling of fear. Everything fits right in just like the word of God said it. Everything began with a dream where God showed me better than a gold lode and I never turned back since. For me the end of this lode is God and the lode is the kingdom of heaven." "What is the kingdom of heaven exactly?" "Only Matthew talked about it. Matthew is the only one as an apostle who touched me with his writing among the four gospels." "What are you saying there?" "The truth. Go read if you don't mind the names of Jesus' apostles in Matthew 10. There is no Mark, there is no Luke and there are too many lies and contradictions in the gospel of John to be from Jesus' John, the apostle. The gospel of John is the very best example of what Jesus described in the parable of the weeds. Just like the weeds over grow the wheat, the lies over grow the truth. This John has even made Jesus a liar in his gospel.

See what is written in John 8, 44 and John 8, 56. Be careful when you read this. 8, 44. 'You belong to your father, the devil and you want to carry out your father's desire. He was a murderer from the beginning, not holding to the truth, for there is no truth in him. When he speaks, he speaks his native language, for he is a liar and the father of lies.'

See also John 8, 39. 'If you were Abraham's children.' Said this Jesus. 'Then you would do the things Abraham did.'

This here is in the same conversation in John 8, 56. 'Your father Abraham rejoiced at the thought of seeing my day; he saw it and he was glad.'

We cannot have for father the devil and Abraham at the same time; it is a total none sense. No, the John of Jesus didn't write such a thing, such stupidity, simply because Jesus, the true prophet never said such a thing and made such of an error. There are a lot of those lies and contradictions in the gospel of John. This is the same liar who said Jesus was killed by the Jews; so he is the enemy of the Jews and the enemy of the Jews is the enemy of God. Especially that we know Jesus was actually killed by the Romans and they were under the orders of Pilate, a Roman governor. This too is according to the Scriptures. See also what Paul said in 1 Thessalonians 2, 14-15. 'You suffered from your own countrymen the same thing those churches suffered from the Jews, who killed the Lord Jesus and the prophets and drove us out. They displease God and are hostile to all men.'

This is got to be the most racist phrase in the whole Bible and it is from Paul. If this is not anti-Semitic, what is it? I would rather say that Paul and men like him are enemies of the Jews. If Jesus was killed by Jews they got to be Jews like Paul.

See Matthew 20, 19. 'And will turn him to the Gentiles to be mocked and flogged and crucified.'

Jesus didn't lie and neither did Matthew. See Matthew 27, 27. 'Then the governor's soldiers (Romans) took Jesus into the Praetorium and gathered the whole company of soldiers around him.'

See also Matthew 27, 31. 'Then they led him away to crucify him.'

The Jews were executing by stoning, not by crucifixion. See the stories of the adulteress and of Stephen. The Roman were executing by crucifixion. Jesus was killed by Gentiles, by the hands of the Romans and not by the Jews like Paul, the liar said. Paul was a liar and so was the John of Paul.

Hitler told the very same lie, telling his people they have to kill the Jews because they were the ones who killed Jesus, the Saviour. Hitler got his people excited about it and he was blessed by Rome for doing so.

What a shame that people can't see the truth!" "You seem to be a lot against this Paul and his John?" "I am against the liars; especially when they are lying about the word of God and they contradict Jesus' messages and other God's prophets.

This is terrible, because they have created the hatred against the nation of Israel, against the Jews that is ongoing still today. Jesus told us to be careful when we'll see the abomination in the holy place that causes desolation. It is written in Matthew 24, 15. Well, I saw the abominations in the Holy Bible (holy place) and I am desolated and I was careful to what I was reading.

Everything is right there under our eyes. I have to admit though that the lies were hidden cleverly and like many thousands people I was blinded and cheated too by the religions and their spokesmen for a long time. I am very blessed though, because God opened my eyes and He delivered me from evil and He allowed me to see, to believe and to accept the truth.

Here are the three beings we need to enter the kingdom of heaven. Only the truth will set us free. We have to be able to see it, we have to be able to believe it and we have to be able to accept it. These are the most important three beings of our life. Then the recipe to see the kingdom of heaven is very simple and I repeat it. It comes from God through Jesus, the prophet God chose to let us know about it. It is written in Matthew 22, 35-40. 'One of them, an expert in the law, tested Jesus with this question: 'Teacher, which is the greatest commandment in the Law?' Jesus replied; 'Love the Lord your God with all your heart and with all your soul and with all you mind. This is the greatest commandment. And the second one is like it; love your neighbour as yourself. All the Law and the Prophets hang on these two commandments.' '

It depends also on this recipe if you will enter or not in the kingdom of heaven. There are the children of God who saw it and others, the leaders of the religions are blocking their followers from entering it. They are blinds who lead the blinds just like Jesus said it. What a horrific crime!

Here is what Jesus said to Paul and to the ones alike. See Matthew 23, 33. 'You snakes! You brood of vipers! How will you escape being condemned to hell?'

See also Matthew, 23, 13. 'But woe to you, scribes and Pharisees, hypocrites, (priests, bishops, archbishops, cardinals, popes and pastors and all of Paul's products) because you shut off the kingdom of heaven from people, for you don't enter it yourselves, nor do you allow those who are entering to go in.'

You have to note here that Jesus didn't condemn the Scribes and the Pharisees, the churches leaders, but he asked them how they could escape the judgement of hell." "Isn't it a sin to get upset and call people's names like Jesus spoke about it in Matthew 5, 22? 'But I say to you that every one who is angry with his brother shall be guilty before the court; and who ever say to his brother, you good for nothing, should be guilty before the high court; and who ever says, you fool, shall be guilty enough to go into the fiery hell.'

I'm talking about snakes here and brood of vipers." "Do you really think the hypocrites and the liars; especially the ones who lie about the word of God are Jesus' brothers?" "I will never win against you." "The truth will win over the lie, this I know.

Now, if the Scribes, the Pharisees, the churches' leaders, the hypocrites and the liars can shut down the kingdom of heaven in people's face with their lies and their people brain's washing and they don't enter themselves, this means then that the Jesus' disciples with the truth, with the word of God can enter it and allow the ones who listen to them like you do to enter it too. I know that I see it and I live in it." "You have a lot of luck." "You too, because you have the chance to listen to the truth just like the Jesus' disciples did it.

Although there are a lot of people who fall before the threats of death and who can blame them? I certainly don't, because I really don't know how I will react before such a situation. I only know that I pray God with all my heart to give me the strength and the courage to stand firm facing evil and death. Only God has the power to keep me with Him and maybe the angels can help. Jesus said it: 'The spirit is willing but the body is weak.'

I hope my language is pure and simple; so everyone who will read this book will understand me or else understand the word of God and all of Jesus' messages." "It is true that all of Jesus' apostles fell before the danger and this beginning with Peter." "This though was the will of God for them to fall that day." "What are you saying there? As if God wanted for the Jesus' disciples to fall. That's a good one" "This is the truth my friend. If they didn't all fall that day we would have next to nothing from God's word. They would all have been crucified with Jesus and most of his messages too." "Hay, I never thought of this, but this is true. At least there would have been a huge risk." "Jesus' three years of his ministry would have been wasted. I don't think God would have liked to see his servant wasted his life for nothing. He doesn't waste his time with me either, because I do what ever He asks from me to do." "How do you know this is from God?" "Because I know that what I'm doing is good and nothing good is coming from the devil." "I admit it, you have a good point there, because you always speak in favour of Jesus and God." "This is because the Lord is my God and Jesus is my director, my Messiah. I listen to Him and I know this is pleasing to Him.

So, I was saying that God's children know the will of their Father, his laws and his commandments. The children of God know the Sabbath day is the last day of the week and not the first day and we have to sanctify it. The others follow and listen to their god too, but they don't follow the God of Israel, the One I follow; otherwise they would know God's will. They love their god with all of their heart too, but which god is he? The children of the true God know also that He doesn't want his children to eat pork. See Isaiah 66, 17. 'Those who consecrate and purify themselves to go in the gardens in the midst of those who eat the flesh of pigs and rats and other abominable things—they will meet their end together.' Declares the Lord.'

This is most likely because pork meat causes cancer just like rats and mice would do. They are vermin and either you cook it or not it is still vermin. I know one thing for sure and this is pork is full of parasites and I also know that parasites cause cancer. If it wasn't for the nitrate they put in this meat ham would be green and bacon would be grey. This would not be too appetizing, to me at least. Isn't it cancer the biggest killer in the world? There are fifteen million people who die every year killed by cancer. What did we just read in Isaiah 66, 17? 'They will meet their end together declares the Lord.'

There is one person who dies every second in the world caused by cancer. How many of them eat pork? There is one person who dies every six seconds in the world because of hunger. Jesus said the devil is a murderer from the beginning. It is because of the wickedness of the people in the world that so many die. And do you know why? Because God said: 'Be fruitful, multiply and feel up the earth.'

Anything is good for the devil to contradict God. Let's turn to God and He will turn to us.

One way or the other; if God has forbidden his children to eat pork it is because He had a very good reason and if his children don't listen to Him, then it is just too bad for them, but this is not God's fault. It is very sad though that so many innocent people die in the process because they don't know. Besides, apparently pork meat is the flesh that resembled the most the human flesh and according to the world record book pig is the most intelligent of all the farm's animals and man is supposed to be the smartest.

Is it possible that most of the people are cannibals?" "Do you mean you don't eat ham or pork bacon?" "Not since I became a true child of God. When we love God with all our heart, all of our soul and with all of our thoughts it is actually easy to give our bacon to our dog. This is what I did with the bacon they put on my plate at the restaurant. But what do you think of everything I say?" "I must say that I learn a lot from you. It is even staggering at times." "I told you before that the truth is often shocking; especially if we are not open to it.

When we have God as a Father we have thoughts and ideas that are coming from Him most of the time. Jesus showed it to us in Matthew 16, 16-17. 'Simon Peter answered, "You are the Christ, the Son of the living God." Jesus replied, "Blessed are you, <u>Simon son of Jonah</u>, for this was not revealed to you by man, but by my Father in heaven." '

Do you know now what this all mean? This means it was the Holy Spirit who was speaking through the mouth of Peter and Peter didn't have to wait for Jesus to die, to resurrect and to be glorified before the Holy Spirit comes in the picture. See also Matthew 10, 20. 'For it will not be you speaking, but the Spirit of your Father speaking through you.'

Of course here I make reference to what John wrote in John 15, 26. 'When the Counselor comes, whom <u>I will send</u> to you from the Father, the Spirit of truth who goes out from the Father, he will testify about me.'

Let me tell you that the Father who is in heaven didn't have and He doesn't have to wait for anyone; especially this Jesus to send his Spirit into the world, but I hope that by now you understood that the Jesus in this John is an impostor, a fake, a demon to deceive you. It is not the son of God or angels or any prophets who send God's Spirit to people, but God Himself, no matter what this guy in the gospel of John said.

This also means the Jesus' disciples were also sons of God. The same thing goes for all the people who do the will of God, the Father who is in heaven; which means follow his laws. On the other hand the devil can also speak through you and we have the evidence a few paragraphs farther in Matthew 16, 23. 'Jesus turned and said to Peter; "Get behind me Satan! You are a stumbling block to me; you don't have in mind the things of God, but the things of men." '

Note here that Jesus didn't call Peter Satan, but was ordering Satan to come out of Peter. This was not the first time Jesus chased a demon away from a man.

I underlined above; Simon son of Jonah. Let's go see whose son Peter is in John 1, 42. 'Jesus looked at him and said, "You are Simon son of John. You will be called Cephas." (Which translated, is Peter)'

This is what I found in the New International Bible and in the Gideon Bible, the New American Standard Bible.

In those days John and Jonah were two very distinct names.

One day in British Columbia, more precisely in Westbank one man was tormenting me and was arguing everything I was saying about the word of God. Since he would not stop contradicting me I was getting exasperated and I asked him to go away. I couldn't believe at what speed he did just that. It was just like God had shut off his mouth and sent him on his way as if there was nothing more to do with this individual.

So, I think thoughts and ideas are from elsewhere and they are spirits, because we know they exist, but no one can see or touch them. We also know too now they can be divine or devilish and this is according to what Jesus said to Peter.

One morning while I was still in bed many thoughts for some very good phrases came to my mind for this book I'm writing. I was really enjoying it and I was stretching my time to get some more when suddenly the need of the morning pulled me out of bed. After I was done I took a pen and paper and, I could not remember a single thing. They might come back one day, who knows?

One more time I realized that my thoughts and my ideas don't really belong to me; that they are either given or loaned to me and we have to be grateful when we get some good ones. The only thing I could remember after a little while was about the three beings we need to enter the kingdom of heaven." "This must have made you sad." "Yes and no; if God wants me to get them back He will give me them again. I could tell you that I went back to bed and I tried to put myself in the same kind of mood trying to get those ideas back, but this was to no avail." "Do you mean that we cannot control our thoughts and our ideas?" "This is exactly what I'm telling you." "So, this means we are not responsible for the bad thoughts and the bad ideas we get?" "No, but we are responsible of what we are doing with them. You are free to accept or to reject them. It is your choice. If you love God with all of your heart you will reject all the bad thoughts and you will take advantage of the good ones and you will make others take advantage of them too. Take for example this book I'm writing, God gave me the idea about it, but it was my choice to write it or not.

I got an idea lately that could make me the richest man on the world within ten years; me who has never looked for wealth. It was not my intention to pursue this idea, but the more I thought about it, the more I understood God's plan to tell all of the nations about the kingdom of heaven. I might need a bit of money just to get my book on the market; especially if I cannot find a publisher who wants to do it. Now, this idea I'm talking about will be very historical. I would go as far as saying it will be just as historical or more as the story of the tour of Babel. I'm talking about an income of many billions of dollars a year. I would put many thousands people to work and not only for an important work, but also a work which is very interesting and pleasant. It is an idea that will go all around the world, in all the nations and all the nations will understand each other." "You're getting to be more and more intriguing." "God's mysteries are numerous, but He said He will publish things hidden since the beginning of the world. It is written in Matthew 13, 35. 'I will open my mouth in parables; I will utter things hidden since the creation of the world.' "

"Isn't it a bad thing to be rich?" "A bad person could do a lot of harm with a lot of money, but on the other hand a good person can do a lot of good with a lot of money. This upset me when I hear on the news that a rich man paid millions of dollars for a collection item like a picture frame. God allowed some people to get rich, many of them who were born naked and poor. He also said it was necessary scandals happen, but woe to the ones by whom they happen. It is written in Matthew 18, 7.

Money gives men the power to do things; it is up to everyone to use this power to do something good." "I never heard anyone to talk like you do." "I think they are rare the Jesus' disciples nowadays and I never met one yet either." "If there are some out there they are quiet." "We cannot forget their lives are in danger continually and dead they are no use to anyone." "You don't seem to be too afraid to say what you have to say?" "No, but the risk for danger is not any less because of it and I am still being careful to whom I talk to. Everyone I talk to about the truth may be a threat to me just like it was for Jesus and for Louis Riel.

CHAPTER 8

If you don't mind I'll get back to the kingdom of heaven now. Do you know it is only mentioned in Matthew and no where else?" "I didn't know about this, but how come?" "I told you that Matthew is the only Jesus' apostle among the four Gospel of the New Testament. The kingdom of heaven is mentioned thirty-two times in Matthew according to my findings and I could not find it anywhere else." "It is kind of strange, isn't it?" "Not really, especially when one understood what really happened." "What happened according to you?" "According to me Matthew reported the real facts, the real stories he lived through with Jesus and the others unscrupulously tried to imitate Matthew adding and subtracting many facts and also changing the signification of many of Jesus' messages." "These are serious accusations, don't you think?" "Maybe so, but I have very good reasons to say this.

I'm talking here about things I found in the gospel of Mark, in Luke and in John, which I will talk about a bit later. So, I was saying that I found thirty-two times in Matthew only where the kingdom of heaven is mentioned. In Mark the kingdom of God is mentioned many times." "This is right, but isn't it the same thing?" "Not at all!" "Explain, because I don't understand this." "The kingdom of God is not of this world, but the kingdom of heaven is here on the earth." "Wow, now I am more confused than ever." "I will try to enlighten you with the best of my knowledge. For what I know the kingdom of God will exist only from the time the devil will be chained forever;

when he will be eliminated from the world. On the other hand the kingdom of heaven is on earth but aside from the world. The world is the kingdom of the devil." "I still don't understand." "I sure hope you will before I'm done with this chapter. I will enumerate a number of verses where Jesus is talking about this famous kingdom of heaven with the hope this will help you to understand. See Matthew 3, 2. 'Repent, for the kingdom of heaven is near.'

It was very near alright, because Jesus, the word of God was about to show up.

See Matthew 4, 17. 'From that time Jesus began to preach, "Repent, for the kingdom of heaven is near." '

Now, this happened almost two thousands years ago. Jesus was certainly not talking about a kingdom that will be there at the end of the world. Jesus was talking about the kingdom that was near him alright; he was talking about the word of God which is in him. Repent, get rid of your sins. It is like a fish that was just clean from its guts. It is clean and good.

Let's continue with Matthew 5, 3. 'Blessed are the poor in spirit, for theirs is the kingdom of heaven.'

What can we blame on the mental retarded people, the one who are without any intelligence? We cannot even blame them for their crimes, even the worst ones like murders and even less their sins. This is why many criminals are faking madness trying to get away with their crime. This was something an honest man like Louis Riel couldn't do. Louis Riel could have used this excuse, because he was locked up as a nut case before and his own lawyers have insisted to use it for his defence. Louis Riel energetically refused to use that excuse. He would rather die physically than spiritually and be with God.

See Matthew 5, 10. 'Blessed are those (like Louis Riel) who are persecuted because of righteousness, for theirs is the kingdom of heaven.'

Jesus doesn't talk about the future here. The kingdom of heaven is theirs now and not in I don't know how many years.

Believe it, it is not the sons of the devil who will be persecuted by men for justice or for the word of God.

See Matthew 5, 19. 'Anyone who breaks one of the least of these commandments and teaches others to do the same will be called the least in the kingdom of heaven, but whoever practices and teaches these commands will be called great in the kingdom of heaven.'

Nothing can be clearer than this." "Now I begin to understand. So you are great in the kingdom of heaven, because contrary to Paul, you practice and you teach to follow the Law of God, the commandments, according to this message from Jesus anyway." "Thanks for realizing it and I am very happy about it." "But what will happen to Paul who eliminate the whole Law and said that we are not under the Law anymore?" "The least it could happen to him is he will be called the least in the kingdom of heaven. We'll see a bit farther what Jesus said about men like him.

See Matthew 5, 20. 'For I tell you that unless your righteousness surpasses that of the Pharisees (like Paul was) and the teachers of the law, you will certainly not enter the kingdom of heaven.'

There you are; this is the answer of your previous question. We have to be at least honest and righteous to enter the kingdom of heaven if we are not crazy." "This is very interesting, but how did you see all of these things no one else seem to talk about?" "I just listened to the one who is telling the truth and nothing but the truth. Everything that contradicts Jesus and God is antichrist and anti-God. We will find other answers as we go farther.

See Matthew 7, 21. "Not everyone who says to me, 'Lord, Lord,' will enter the kingdom of heaven, but only he who does the will of my Father in Heaven."

Now, this is crystal clear enough too. The one who does the will of the Father in heaven is the one who is under the Law of God and obeys or follows his commandments.

You can see for yourself that Paul said the exact opposite of Jesus and you can read it in Romans 10, 13. "Everyone who calls on the name of the Lord will be saved."

Paul said the exact opposite of Jesus again, which one do you believe?

It is obvious that we are better to know the will of God." "You said it and I'd be better listening to you all the way. It is very interesting and intriguing. I would even say more, it is fascinating. You must have a gift to do all this." "If I have a gift it is the gift of wanting the truth to come out and maybe a bit of the gift of seeing. In the ancient time they were calling the prophets seers. I tell you one more time, if I see it is because God speaks to me and I listen to the One who is the light and I get enlightened. When Jesus said he is the light of the world, this is because he is the word of God and since God said He will put his word in the mouth of his servant Jesus, a prophet like Moses who will be coming from the brothers of Israel; he is the one to listen to. Let's get back to our sheep of the kingdom of heaven now.

See Matthew 8, 11. 'I say to you that many will come from the East and the West and will take their places at the feast with Abraham, Isaac and Jacob in the kingdom of heaven.'

See, Jesus was talking for years to come. I just know that I will have my place too at this table and be sure of one thing, Jesus will be there too. In fact I write it in one of my hymns called; Praises To My Lord.

See what Jesus said in his instructions to his apostles in Matthew 10, 7. 'As you go, preach this message: 'The kingdom of heaven is near.'

See Matthew 11, 11. 'I tell you the truth: Among those born of women (Jesus was) there are not risen anyone greater than John the Baptist; yet he who is least in the kingdom of heaven is greater than he.'

This is not an easy one, because Jesus was also born from a woman and as far as I know he was raised too. See Deuteronomy 18, 18. 'God said: 'I will raise up for them a prophet like you, Moses.' '

I think Jesus was saying that at one time John the Baptist was the greatest, but might have diminished before he died or else Jesus never really said this. I sure don't think John the Baptist was greater than Jesus and I'm also sure Jesus never said he was not born from a woman. I also know that Jesus' enemies tried to make people believe Jesus was not human.

The way Jesus spoke in this verse; he told us that even John the Baptist was not a saint even if he was the greatest. I think that John the Baptist didn't recognize the kingdom of heaven, which is in the word of God. He, John the Baptist who baptized Jesus sent his disciples to Jesus asking him if he was the one to come or if he should expect another one. This is because John the Baptist was not yet in the kingdom of heaven and he still had doubts about Jesus, the Messiah. Anyway, Jesus knew that John the Baptist was less than the least in the kingdom of heaven and I'm sure he had his reasons to say so. Maybe it was just because this John lacked faith.

The next verse is also important to help us understand that the kingdom of heaven is here on earth. See Matthew 11, 12. 'From the days of John the Baptist until now, the kingdom of heaven has been forcefully advancing, and forceful men lay hold on it.'

Believe it or not, the forceful men or any devilish men won't be able to lay hold on the kingdom of God, because in this kingdom there will be no madness. The word of God will be in every man and woman's heart and God will be the God of everyone. See Jeremiah 31, 33. "This is the covenant I will make with the house of Israel after that time," declares the Lord. "I will put my law in their minds and write it in their hearts. I will be their God, and they will be my people."

This will be the kingdom of God, not the kingdom of heaven and there will be nothing bad in it, especially no forceful men.

See Matthew 13, 11. 'Jesus replied, "The knowledge of the secrets of the kingdom of heaven has been given to you, but not to them." '

This is the same reason why you are listening and I speak to you. This is the work of Jesus that is continuing. I sure hope that with you too the seed will fall in good soil and produce one hundred to one or more." "I'm not very quick, but I understand more and more as I listen to you. It does me good to listen to you." "It is nice to hear this and it is always comforting to see someone interested to hear the word of God. This kind of compensate for all the ones who reject it, in fact, there are very few who listen.

See Matthew 13, 24. 'Jesus told them another parable: "The kingdom of heaven is like a man who sowed good seed in his field." '

Does this remind you something?" "It is like you talking to me. I am the soil; I am the field who receives the good seed. The good seed is the word of God you're giving me." "I hope this field will be very fruitful and the owner of this field will know how to eliminate the weeds and throw them in the fire to stop them from spreading. You will have to be careful, because they are numerous men who disguise themselves as angels of heaven. Note that these can be women too. By knowing the truth though you will recognize the liars either they lie conscientiously or not.

The weeds, the lies have been seeded so craftily in the Bible that many people lie without knowing it. I know my sisters do. He is crafty the enemy and it is mentioned in a few places in the Bible. Look in Genesis 3, 1 and in 2 Corinthians 12, 16.

Do you see? God said; 'You will certainly die if you eat from the central tree.'

The devil told Adam and Eve: 'You will not die, but your eyes will open.'

Adam and Eve didn't die physically, but they die spiritually, this is what sin does to us.

Jesus said, see Matthew 5, 17-18. 'Do not think that I have come to abolish the Law or the Prophets; I have not come to abolish them but to fulfill them. I tell you the truth, until heaven and earth disappear, not the smallest letter, not the least stroke of a pen, will by any means disappear from the Law until everything is accomplished.'

See now what the crafty one said in Ephesians 2, 15-16. 'By abolishing in his flesh the Law with its commandments and regulations. His purpose was to create in himself one new man out of the two, thus making peace, and in this one body to reconcile both of them to God through the cross, by which he put to death their hostility.'

Jesus died on the cross almost two thousands years ago and the hostility still exists today. Jesus said that for as long as the earth and heaven exist, not the least stroke of a pen will disappear from the Law or from the commandments. On the other hand Paul, the crafty one said that Jesus abolished the Law with its commandments by dying on the cross. I am sure Jesus didn't lie; this means the other one did.

Do you see how the devil operates? This is always the same pattern for the devil; he is always contradicting God and his servants.

God also said something about his Law and commandments. See Jeremiah 31, 36. 'Only if these decrees vanish from my sight declares the Lord, will the descendants of Israel ever cease to be a nation before me.'

And did they ever try to make the nation of Israel disappeared, especially Rome and its followers. But the hand of God is on Israel and all the efforts from its enemies to destroy it failed anyway and always will.

See Matthew 13, 31. 'Jesus told them another parable: "The kingdom of heaven is like a mustard seed, which a man took and planted in his field."

Do you know that this seed God put in me is growing above the highest mountains of the world and all the birds of the shies will come and find shelter on it? They will in turn carry this seed and put it in a good soil that will produce more wheat; spreading the truth across the world and eliminate the weeds, the lies which hurt the production.

See Matthew 13, 33. "The kingdom of heaven is like yeast that a woman took and mixed into a large amount of flower until it worked all through the dough."

"This one is not easy to understand either." "I got to give you this, I agree. I had a hard time to understand it too. This is what I'm doing with you, meaning producing disciples until all the nations know the word of God, the truth. The goal of the beast, of the antichrist is to kill as many people as possible and this before they receive the word of God.

This is why I say I risk my life by doing what I do. One member of the beast gave us an example in Titus 1, 11. 'They must be silenced.'

Do you know how we keep people quiet? It is a term frequently used by the mafia. To keep someone silenced is to eliminate him. This letter was from Paul to one of his disciples named Titus." "I'm I mistaking or this Paul had some strange ways for a man who was supposed to be an apostle?" "You're not mistaking at all, because according to what I found Paul is contradicting Jesus and God hundreds of times. But the worst of all is that basically all of the Christian churches are based on his teaching." "This is very scary." "You said it, but don't be scared, be careful. The danger is less when we know the enemy.

See Matthew 13, 44. 'The kingdom of heaven is like a treasure hidden in a field. When a man found it, he hid it again, and then in his joy went and sold all he had and bought that field.' "

"Here again, this is something I don't understand." "This is very simple my friend. Once we have found this water of life, the bread from heaven, the truth, when we are fed with this bread from heaven we were looking for, for so long, we can give everything we have to make it our own and live in the kingdom of heaven. Nothing matters anymore as much as spreading this seed, this truth, even at the cost of our life. This is what happened to Jesus, to his apostles and to many of his disciples and to Louis Riel also. We have the proof today, they have eternal life. They will live forever, just like Jesus promised them.

Here is another very important message from Jesus in Matthew 13, 43. 'Then the righteous will shine like the sun in the kingdom of their Father.'

Here Jesus is talking about the future; which is about the kingdom of God and not about the kingdom of heaven, which is now while we live.

The kingdom of God will be after the judgement for the righteous who have listened and followed Jesus.

First, the righteous have God as a Father, like Jesus said it. Jesus who often spoke about the kingdom of heaven here didn't speak about it, but he talked about the kingdom of the Father." "Do you know why?" "Here is my explanation. In the kingdom of God there is nothing bad. There are no more forceful men advancing or having hold on the kingdom of heaven like there were, because the Jesus' angels pulled away all the weeds, all the wicked and threw them in the fiery furnace. The wicked people that Jesus and many of his disciples warned and yet in many ways and they kept sinning, believing the lies that the blood of Jesus, his death on the cross could save them. If Jesus death alone could save the sinners who believe in this lie; Jesus wouldn't have had to teach anybody. Jesus would just simply have said: 'Here I am, the Son of God, I give my life to save you and all you have to do is to believe it. You can sin all you want, all your sins belong to me.'

In fact, this is what the devil did, this is what he said. God said his servant will save many with his knowledge, not with his death on the cross. See Isaiah 53, 11. 'With his knowledge my righteous servant will justify many.'

But about this too the devil contradicted God.

See Matthew 13, 45-46. 'Again the kingdom of heaven is like a merchant looking for fine pearls. When he found one of great value, he went away and sold everything he had and bought it.'

Jesus had an extraordinary way to tell us that there was nothing better, nothing nicer, nothing more important than the truth, the word of God, which leads us to live in the kingdom of heaven. I can assure you that I have never experienced as much happiness, as much personal satisfaction before I began working to accomplish the will of my Father who is in heaven. It is almost unexplainable. I can also tell you the weeping and the gnashing of teeth are not for the children of God.

When Matthew has discovered Jesus he left everything on the spot to follow Jesus. Matthew knew right then he had just discovered the most precious pearl on earth. Although the pastors of the Baptist Evangelical Church where I used to go asked me if I really knew who Matthew was? One of them said Matthew was a vulgar tax collector for the Romans.

I told them then that they didn't do as much as Matthew did for the kingdom of heaven. Matthew left everything behind to follow Jesus and it's true they didn't do as much. Matthew left the money; they on the contrary picked up money. This got me my first persecutions coming from the Jesus' enemies.

See Matthew 13, 47-48. 'Once again, the kingdom of heaven is like a net that was let down into the lake and caught <u>all kind of fish</u>. <u>When it was full</u>, the fishermen pulled it up on the shore. Then they sat down and collected the good fish in baskets, but threw the bad away.'

Did you see the sense of this phrase? Jesus is talking at the present time; 'The kingdom of heaven <u>is</u> like.'

Jesus didn't say, it was or it will be, but is like. This is the present time of each of us and this was true at his time, it is true for our time as it will be for every century until the end time.

Did you understand this message?" "It is the same as many others about the kingdom of heaven; we have to clean our acts in our lives of all wickedness." "This is true in parts only." "What is the difference then?" "There are all kinds of fish." "What is this mean?" "This means there are in the kingdom of heaven people from all over, from all nations and of all races. They are coming from the West and from the East, from the North and from the South. It is our duty to make disciples from all the nations." "Why did you include me in this statement? How can you tell I will participate?" "If you weren't interested you would have stopped asking me questions longtime ago." "I am very lucky to have you." "I wish you just as much.

There was another important message in this statement; can you tell me what it is?" "No, I don't know. I thought everything was said about it." "The good fish were put in a basket, but the bad were thrown away." "What is this means?" "This will be the conclusion of the kingdom of heaven; when the Jesus' angels will gather the good people to the kingdom of God and the bad ones away in the fiery furnace, in hell." "When will this conclusion be?" "When the net will be full; when God knows no more people will enter the kingdom of heaven.

See Matthew 13, 52. 'Jesus said to them; "Therefore every teacher of the Law who has been instructed about the kingdom of heaven is like the owner of a house who brings out of his storeroom new treasures as well as old." '

This might just be a bad translation. Jesus often said we have to sell everything to buy the precious pearl. He also said not to accumulate treasures and where our treasure is will be our heart and it is almost impossible for a rich man to enter the kingdom of heaven." "It is true that this message might be confusing; especially because the Jesus' apostles just said they understood." "This message doesn't look like the others, but when I thought about it a second time, this most likely means we are not to neglect anything we learned, either longtime ago or just lately.

In fact, this is me, the teacher of the Law who knows about the word of God, who was instructed about the kingdom of heaven and I tell you things I have learned latterly and things I have learned longtime ago.

See what Jesus said to Peter in Matthew 16, 19. 'I will give you the keys of the kingdom of heaven; whatever you bind on earth will be bound in heaven, and whatever you loose on earth will be loosed in heaven.'

The leaders of basically all the religions got hold of this declaration from Jesus, especially with the confession, but to deserve this power one has to be like Peter, meaning first to be a Jesus' disciple and second, to preach the truth. All the priests and pastors, all religions leaders who like Paul contradict the Jesus' messages and like Paul did it, they condemned millions of people to hell. They certainly don't have this power. Remember the lean Fridays; the outlaw services on the first day of the week and so many other condemnations.

I know many people who have trouble with the verse 16, 19 of Matthew. I'm not too sure if this is by jealousy or by envy or something else. I know that Peter was the first one chosen by Jesus as an apostle. He was a man who had faith as strong and as solid as rock and it is on this rock Jesus built his church, one church. For sure Jesus needed such a man to continue his ministry. A man who had enough faith at one point to walk on the water.

All the apostles had to have a strong faith to continue spreading the word of God at the risk of losing their lives. When it comes to the keys of the kingdom of heaven, these are nothing else than all the instructions, all the messages Jesus gave his disciples. These are the same messages I give to you today. It is the word of God, the truth that opens the doors of the kingdom of heaven. When it comes to bind and to loose anything on earth, this is very simple; because with the Law of God and the word of God a person has the necessary tools he needs to teach everyone what ever it takes to enter the kingdom of heaven." "Do you mean you are holding these keys too?" "Don't you get an answer to all of your questions? The keys of the kingdom of heaven and the keys of the hidden mysteries from the beginning of the world are the same keys." "Do you know that what you're saying there is totally amazing?" "The things that are very amazing my friends are the revelations given to me from God.

See Matthew 18, 1-4. 'At the time the disciples came to Jesus and asked, "Who is the greatest in the kingdom of heaven?" Jesus called a little child and had him stand among them. And he said: "I tell you the truth, unless you change and become like little children, you will not enter the kingdom of heaven. Therefore, whoever humbles himself like this child is the greatest in the kingdom of heaven." '

This is another confirmation that to enter the kingdom of heaven we have to be humble enough to repent and be as clean as a child; a child who is greater than John the Baptist. We have to be as clean as a fish ready to be eaten. We cannot enter this kingdom with sins. The kingdom of heaven is only for the children of God, the God of the living, the God of those who live their lives without sin.

What can we blame the children for even those who were not baptized?" "Do you mean they can go to heaven without being baptized?" "Jesus said it. They already are in the kingdom of heaven. This is true too to the adults who are really retarded of course. The others have to repent and turn away from their sins to enter it, simple as that. Anyone who says the opposite of Jesus is antichrist." "What is this mean exactly to be antichrist?" "This is to say and do the contrary of what Jesus, the Christ has taught. There are many of them right there in the Bible and many of them who follow them as well." "But aren't we all responsible for the sins of Adam and Eve?" "I just wonder who invented such a myth. Go read Ezekiel 18, 18." "'But the father will die for his own sin, because he practiced extortion, robbed his brother and did what was wrong among his people.'

Understand this right here; dying for his own sin is dying spiritually, not physically. This is the kind of death we can resurrect from with repentance. 'Go and live your life off sin.' Jesus said to the adulteress. The true repentance is exactly what holds back a person to go back to his sin. We cannot mock God forever unpunished. See again Deuteronomy 18, 19. 'If anyone does not listen (and they are many) to my words that the prophet (Jesus) speaks in my name, I Myself will call him to account.'

See Matthew 18, 23. 'Therefore, the kingdom of heaven is like a king who wanted to settle accounts with his servants.'

In the kingdom of heaven, contrary to what is done in the world we are treated fairly and according to our deeds." "But I saw somewhere in the Bible the exact opposite." "If it is the opposite, it is certainly not from Jesus or from one of his disciples. But I think I know what you are referring to. See Galatians 3, 6-9. 'Consider Abraham: "He believed God, and it was credited to him as righteousness." Understand then, that those who believe are children of Abraham. The Scripture foresaw that God would justify the Gentiles <u>by faith</u>, and announced the gospel in advance to Abraham.'

Ho, this kind of looks like the truth for the ones who are not aware of the true God's statement about Abraham. But take a good look if you will at James 2, 19. 'You believe that there is one God. Good! Even the <u>demons believe that</u>—and shudder.'

Are the demons justified by their faith Paul and his followers?

See now what James, Jesus' brother had to say about faith, James 2, 24. 'You see that a person is justified by what he does and not by faith alone.'

Like Paul said. I like James a lot, mainly for telling us the truth. We can also read a message from Jesus about faith and deeds. See Matthew 11, 19. 'The Son of Man came eating and drinking and they say, 'Here is a glutton and a drunkard, a friend of tax collectors and "sinners." ' But wisdom is proved right by his actions.'

Words of Jesus! See also and it is very important Jesus in Matthew 16, 27. 'For the Son of Man is going to come in his Father's glory with <u>his angels</u> and then, he will reward each person according to (his faith, no, no, but to) <u>what he has done</u>.'

Let me show you what the demons were thinking about Jesus and they too believe in Jesus and in God. See Mark 1, 23-24. 'Just then a man in there synagogue who was possessed by an evil spirit cried out, "What do you want with us, Jesus of Nazareth? Have you come to destroy us? I know who you are—the Holy One of God." '

The demons know it, but many people don't.

See another thing Jesus said about deeds in Matthew 5, 16. 'In the same way, let your light shine before men, that they may see your <u>good deeds</u> and praise your Father in heaven.'

Faith can't be seen for it is invisible. Jesus really said; "So they can see your deeds." Not your faith that is totally useless without deeds like James said.

I'm pretty sure my books will be read by many, many people.

Is this answering your question?" "You seem to have an answer to everything." "There is something else. You have seen that Paul said all the nations are blessed because of <u>Abraham's faith</u>, didn't you?" "This is what is written in Paul's letter to the Galatians 3, 6-9, yes." "See now what God Himself said about this in Genesis 26, 4-5. 'I will make your descendants as numerous as the stars in the sky and I will give them all these lands, and through your offspring all nations on earth will be blessed, because Abraham (believed, no, no) obeyed Me and kept my requirements, my commands, my decrees and my laws.'

Should you believe Paul or God? People who believe Paul are lost. The wake up time is here.

See Matthew 19, 12. 'For some are eunuchs because they were born that way; others were made that way by men and others have renounced marriage because of the kingdom of heaven.' "

"Not too many people can understand the message in this verse. I know I don't understand it at all." "You have no idea of what this is all about?" "Not at all!" "There are people who would like to enter the kingdom of heaven at all cost, but their sexuality is too strong and forbids them to do it. One term or one expression often employed in French is this one: 'More tail than head.' Their sexual hormones forbid them to live without sin." "This is direct enough, thanks." "No problem!

We have to understand here too that the religions have made sins where there were none. It is not more of a sin to scratch your ass than it is to scratch your nose. Our body belongs to us and it is up to us to take care of it the best way we can, no matter what the needs are.

Here is a reference from Jesus about this in Matthew 5, 30. 'If your right hand causes you to sin, cut it off and throw it away. It is better for you to lose one part of your body than for your whole body to go into hell.'

So, it is better for a man to be castrated than to live a life of homosexuality, because this is an abomination. Just remember that adultery is not any better. Another thing to consider in

Jesus' last statement is the fact he said the body in hell and not the soul. This too is on earth. The same thing is true for your right eye. When Jesus said in Matthew 8, 12, 13, 42, 13, 50, 22, 13, 24, 51 and 25, 30, that there will be weeping and gnashing of teeth, this too is impossible in many hundreds degrees, not to say thousands. So this means there will be spiritual and physical sufferings, but on earth." "This is not easy to take, to accept." "Why do you say this? Which is worst, lose you hand, your eye, your testicles or to spend the eternity in hell?" "When we look at it this way; it is losing a part of the body of course." "This is what Jesus said too. On the other hand, if you love God with all of your heart and to the point you are ready to get rid of one part of your body and to become a eunuch, because you want to enter the kingdom of heaven; then you'll find a way with the help of God to fight the demons who are in control of you.

It took me a long time, but today I prefer giving my pork bacon to my dogs rather than eat pork and displeased God. This is the kind of fasting that pleases God. See Isaiah 58, 5-14, especially verse 6. 'Is not this the kind of fasting I have chosen; to loose the chains of injustice and untie the cords of the yoke, to set the oppressed free and break every yoke?'

See Matthew 19, 14. 'Jesus said: "Let the little children come to me, and do not hinder them, for the kingdom of heaven belongs to such as these.'

We have to understand too that when Jesus say; 'Let the little children come to me.' In reality it means; 'Let the little children come to the word of God.' Because this is what Jesus is. It doesn't mean to let the little children come to him as a man. And as I was saying before, what can we blame on children? Not a crime, not a sin and he is humble and spotless.

See Matthew 19, 23. 'Then Jesus said to his disciples: "I tell you the truth, it is hard for a rich man to enter the kingdom of heaven." '

It is not easy at all to leave everything behind, a fortune which is tangible; it is something he can take advantage of, see it, smell it and touch it for something that is as abstracted as the kingdom of heaven, unless we have understood like Matthew did that the kingdom of heaven is the most precious pearl and the greatest value there is.

There is a very good example about this story in Matthew 19, 22.

See Matthew 19, 24. 'Again I tell you, it is easier for a camel to go through the eye of a needle than for a rich man to enter the kingdom <u>of God</u>.'

In one verse Jesus talked abut a rich man and the kingdom of heaven and in the other he talked about the rich man and the kingdom of God. I don't think Jesus made the mistake, but it is a translation mistake in the second case. Although I think it will be hard for a rich man to enter either one. Everyone has to enter the kingdom of heaven before he could enter the kingdom of God anyway.

Did you understand what this means, a camel through the eye of a needle?" "It is clear that a camel can't go through the eye of a needle." "You are absolutely wrong; it is very possible for a camel to do it." "Then you got me more than ever. I really want to believe this, but this is beyond me. The camel has some bones way too big for it to be possible to go through it." "You will understand in a minute. Jesus wasn't talking about a knitting needle but about a door in the city wall they had in those days. To be able to go through it the camel had to get on his knee and get rid of everything he was carrying. This door was also called the needle. We see some imitations of this needle behind some houses and most of the time they go through it to enter the garden. They are symbolic." "You will never cease to impress me. You are ironically incredible." "This last explanation is not of my own and it didn't come to me from heaven, at least I don't think so, but I heard it along the years and I don't remember where and neither how or from whom." "You didn't have to tell me this." "No I know, but remember, I like the truth, honesty, righteousness and frankness, so does my God.

If it is so hard for a rich man to enter the kingdom of heaven it is because his fortune is more important to him than the truth, the word of God and he is too attached to his goods.

See Matthew 20, 1. 'For the kingdom of heaven is like a landowner who went out early in the morning to hire men to work in his vineyard.'

The last one to enter the kingdom of heaven will get just as much as the first one to do so and God wants it this way. That you come to God at the beginning of your life or you come to God at the end of you life, when you come to God you are with God and you'll get the royal treatment. Everything belongs to Him and He does what He wants with it, just like I do what I want with what belongs to me. I don't fear anything about his justice, for He asked us to be fair.

See Matthew 22, 2. 'The kingdom of heaven is like a king who prepared a wedding banquet for his son.'

The invitation from God to his kingdom is for everyone, good or bad, it is up to us to dress decently, with righteousness for his banquet and to deserve to participate. We cannot do it on our own, but with God in our live, everything is possible. The one who has always done right, who has always looked for justice is white and pure and the one who just sincerely repented for his sins after living a life of debauchery is also white and pure; so there is no difference between the two of them. The two of them are children of God." "But never anyone has enplaned this the way you do, not even Jesus, I'm sure of it." "I heard a pastor once saying in his sermon that he didn't believe in this injustice. This was another one of them who didn't know God." "This was a blind man who was leading other blinds and there are big risks they all fall in a pit.

I just received the inspiration from God to inform you, but I never thought, at least I don't think I did, that God was unfair and I never thought this about Jesus either.

See Matthew 23, 13. 'Woe to you, teachers of the Law and Pharisees, you hypocrites! You shut the kingdom of heaven in people faces. You yourselves do not enter, nor will you let those enter who are trying to.'

Woe to you priests and pastors, leaders and hypocrites; you are shutting down the kingdom of heaven to people and you want to stop me who is trying to help them enter it." "You are quite strict towards them, don't you think?" "Jesus was too and so I am, exactly for the same reasons. They held people from the truth and they are still doing this; just to satisfy their own ambitions, their own benefits. You have learned from me more in a few hours than their followers did from them in an entire life and this didn't cost you a penny. This is to follow Jesus' instructions. Who do you think they have followed and still do?" "For what I can deduct, they are following Paul." "You said it. They have followed Paul and they are following Paul, the liar.

See Matthew 24, 14. 'And this gospel of the kingdom will be preached in the whole world as a testimony to all nations, and then the end will come.'

This is a message which tells me my books will travel across the whole world and this in every language." "You sound pretty sure of yourself." "I have reasons to be, because the word of God doesn't lie, this I am convinced of it." "This might be someone else who makes the word of God known through out the world." "This is fine with me if this is the case, I'm not jealous, but this someone else we never heard from him yet. If he exists he is pretty quiet up till now. There is one thing I read in Revelation and this is there are supposed to be two prophets who will torment the inhabitants of the earth just before the end time and I know my books will torment many people. When I say my books, of course I'm talking about what I wrote in them, my knowledge about the word of God. The truth will trouble many people, because a lot of them all they know are the lies." "I must say again that you are right about this one too.

See Matthew 25, 1. 'At the time the kingdom of heaven <u>will be</u> like ten virgins who took their lamps and went out to meet the bridegroom.'

For the first time when Jesus talked about the kingdom of heaven here he talked about the future. I think this will be at the door of the judgement, where the goats will be on one side and the sheep on the other before their destination. Go read Matthew 25 from verse 31 to 46 to see what will happen. If we recall other messages; we have to be ready for that day and not be like the impious of the time of Noah. It is sure best not to wait to the last minutes like the five foolish virgins of this story did. You can lie to yourselves and believe your lies if we want to, but try to fool God will certainly play against you like it did for those five. Many will stay out of the kingdom of God, out of this feast, because they weren't dressed to enter. They didn't repent on time.

There is another very important point in this story; can you tell me what it is?" "No, I don't see it. What is it?" "There were ten virgins?" "Yes, but what is the point?" "How many were saved and how many were lost?" "There were five on each side, but again, what is the point?" "Well, there was fifty per cent on both sides, but this is not the first time Jesus talked about fifty per cent. Take a look in Matthew 24, 40-41. 'Two men will be in a field; one will be taken and the other left. Two women will be grinding with a hand mill; one will be taken and the other left.'

In my opinion when the world has reached the fifty, fifty per cent of integrity and wickedness, when the good will be overpowered by the bad, when the power of the holy people will be broken the end will come. God then would have no more reason to wait any longer. The dice will be thrown and God will have to slice and then God's sword will hit.

The copy of this story in Luke is a bit different. See Luke 17, 34. 'I tell you, on that night two people will be in one bed; one will be taken and the other left.'

In Matthew Jesus talked about two people working in day time and in Luke he talked about two people in bed at night. It is a bit contradicting since God said that what ever He has united let no man separate. I'm sure that God didn't unite two people of the same sex in the same bed. But I know Luke wrote stories he heard about and Matthew has really spent time with Jesus. Luke spoke about two people together in bed without specifying their genders, but if they were two of the same sex, then this will be hundred per cent taken." "What makes you say this?" "Go read Leviticus 20, 13." "'If a man lies with a man as one lies with a woman, <u>both</u> have done what is detestable. They must be put to death; their blood will be on their own heads.' "

"Both of them, this means one hundred per cent. Just know that adultery is not any better." "Does this mean they are condemned?" "The only way they can have a chance to be saved is to repent and to turn away from their sins. If they got caught in the middle of the night with their pants down and have no time to repent, it is just too bad, but it is too late for them just like it was for the five foolish virgins. The call for repentance is launched to all the sinners; it is up to them to listen or to ignore the call. When Jesus said; "Repent for the kingdom of heaven is near." He said it to everybody and he didn't say repent today and sin tomorrow."

"A little while ago you said something that kind of bugs me since." "What is it?" "The fact we only have about twenty years before the final conflict. How can you be so sure?" "But I'm not sure at all about this. I only said this was according to my calculations. I know for sure that God has always been precised to everything He has done and He will be about what ever He still has to do too. If He wasn't the stars in heaven would have started to fall on our heads longtime ago. Besides, Jesus said that all our hairs were counted and wouldn't fall without the Father knowing about it." "But how could you come up with about twenty years left?" "Well, I think the last world conflict will come exactly two thousands years from the time Jesus died on the cross. I think the count down stared at the exact time when the curtain was split in two from top to bottom.

See Matthew 27, 51. 'At the moment the curtain of the temple was torn in two from top to bottom. The earth shook and the rocks split.'

Many people were very scared just before the year 2000 began. I think they had made the wrong calculation." "What will happen?" "We will have a war like we never had before and you know we had some very bad ones." "There must be some other signs for you to talk this way?" "There are many of them." "Can you tell me a few of them?" "Yes, I think one of the biggest ones is mentioned in Matthew 24, 29. 'Immediately after the distress of those days, the sun will be darkened, and the moon will not give its light; the stars will fall from the sky and <u>the heavenly body will be shaken.</u>'

Today people are going on the moon, on the planet Mars and I think they are disturbing other planets as well. Then the love of the most has already cool off. We know this and we also know the knowledge has increased a lot." "What do you think God thinks about the gay marriage?" "I'm pretty sure his anger is inflaming again. Just like I said before; it is certainly not God who unites them. When God had enough of the corruption at the time of Noah He sent the flood to clean up the earth. When God had enough of the corruption of Sodom and Gomorrah He simply reduced them to ashes with all their inhabitants, except for Lot and his family. The drop that will make God mad again I think is not very far. Like I said it; maybe this is around twenty years; which is two thousand years exactly from the death of Jesus on the cross.

There are other signs like this one here. The knowledge will increase and this is done. There is this one which I think involve me personally. See Matthew 24, 14. 'This gospel of the kingdom of heaven shall be preached in the whole world as a testimony to all the nations, and then the end will come.' "

"In another word you will be the one who contributes for this to happen." "If taking parts of the word of God is contributing to the coming of the end time; then you are right to say so and if this means helping to get rid of the bad, getting rid of the devil in the world, then I am very proud to be a participant.

Now I will inform you about a few calculations I made which I think make a lot of sense.

In case you are scare of the end time let me tell you that the end time is the end of the devil's reign and the beginning of

Jesus' reign, the reign of the word of God. Jesus will reign with all of his followers. Jesus is the word of God; so it is the word of God that will reign for a thousand years. I myself have a hard time waiting until then. This shouldn't be too hard since the devil and his angels will be chained for a thousand years as well.

Just think about it for two seconds, nobody to hurt us anymore. This in itself will be hell for the demons. This in itself will be enough to make them weeping and gnashing their teeth, but this will be happiness, peace and paradise for us.

According to the prophets God created the world in six days, (six thousand years) and He rested on the seventh day. One thousand years. See 2 Peter 3, 8.

It is obvious that God couldn't be resting for as long as the devil and his demons were crawling all over the earth.

According to the prophets man is on the earth for almost six thousand years and God largely deserves his rest. All the nations are about to discover the truth and I am very happy to contribute to this gigantic challenge. I have to say that I asked God to use me as He sees me fit for it and I am very happy He trusted me with this challenge."

"But when will he come?" "Only God knows it. According to what Jesus told us he didn't know it himself and this was for a very good reason too, because they would have tortured him to death to find out. This is why Jesus asked us to be ready at all time. I know I am.

I know perfectly well that God always been precised with everything and He has to be too to hold everything in place in the universe. So He will be precised as well with all that has to be done still. If the end comes like I said two thousand years after the death of Jesus I might have a chance to see this coming while I am still alive on this earth. There are many details which make me believe in it.

First we have to read in Daniel which I think is the real Revelation. The angels told him when the end will come. They told him: 'It will be for a time, times and half a time.' See Daniel 12, 7.

179

Let's just say that a time is one thousand years, that times are two thousand years and that half a time is five hundred years. Daniel was there five hundred years before Jesus and Jesus was there almost two thousand years ago. This means that Daniel was there almost twenty-five hundred years ago when he received this message from God or from one of his angels. This is about to make the count. We are getting close to the end of our actual world, the end of the kingdom of the devil. So the reign of the word of God is about to begin. This should happen exactly two thousand thirty-three years from the birth of Jesus. His reign will last one thousand years, which leads us to three thousand five hundred years from when Daniel was told: 'One time, times and half a time.'

In my opinion this is three thousand five hundred years from when Daniel received this message to the kingdom of God. This is quite a precision.

For me I think everything started when God revealed to me the name of the beast and who is the antichrist. So, according to my calculations in about twenty years the sheep will be separated from the goats and the righteous will shine like the sun in the kingdom of their Father. On the other side there will be weeping and gnashing of teeth. May people who have ears to hear can hear and eyes to see can see while they still have time to see. See Matthew 13, 42-43.

There is another calculation I made and I think it is quite impressive. I am talking about the week God took to create the world, including us, the human beings and all the animals. So, it is written that God created the world in six days and He rested on the seventh day, the last day of the week. Now, a lot of people already know that to God a day is like a thousand years and a thousand years are like one day. We have a few references on this subject. One of these is in Psalm 90, 4. 'For a thousand years in your sight are like a day that has just gone by or like a watch in the night.'

There is one more reference in 2 Peter 3, 8. 'But do not forget one thing, dear friends: With the Lord a day is like a thousand years and a thousand years are like a day.'

I have the impression Peter wrote the lines for me and I thank him for it. But we can agree on one thing about all this and this is that for God a day is like a thousand years or a thousand years are like one day.

So this would mean that according to the prophets who were there long before me and what they wrote in the scriptures Adam and Eve were created six thousand years ago. So this means six day for God. His day of rest is about to begin since He couldn't really be resting for as long as the devil and his demons were roving on earth. The day of rest for God will begin the day Satan will be chained for a thousand years with his demons. This is what is written in Revelation 20, 1-2. 'And I saw an angel coming down out of heaven, having the key to the abyss and holding in is hand a great chain. He seized the dragon, that ancient serpent who is the devil, or Satan and bound him for a thousand years.'

Jesus told us too in some sort that God the Father is always at work and He never stopped doing so. See John 5, 17. "My Father is always at his work to this very day and I too, am working."

So what I can get from this message is the Father didn't take his day of rest yet. Jesus had some very good reasons to ask us not to repeat some vain prayers.

Now, six thousand years could very well be 2190 million years, which would be 2,190,000 days multiplied by one thousand years. This would also take us close to the calculations of the scientists of nowadays." "This is absolutely incredible, just unbelievable. I am absolutely sure now that you had some revelations from up there. You can't just pull this all out of a hat like a magician does." "What a magician pulls out of a hat is nothing but illusions. I am telling you real things. Everything I say to you is genuine, it can be verify and it is calculable.

This is what I am doing." "I can see this, but I think the beast will react violently." "I'm not afraid, at least for now and I already put my life in the hands of God. The churches are not in a hurry to preach the good news, the truth and the word of God, because they know their end. They have accumulated gold and money, properties of millions of dollars thinking they might have enough to fight against God. There will be tribulation; there is no doubt in my mind. God could if He wanted to cover the whole earth with one hundred feet thick of snow, which would paralyse everything. He could also bury complete countries with one breath from his nose. He could destroy a whole continent with only one tornado. One has to be as proud and as malicious as the devil to think he can fight against and beat God.

One day is coming and it is not very far when the help to the victims of a disaster won't be there for them anymore, because there will be too many catastrophes.

There is another reason I think why they said Jesus is God and this is his answer when Pilate asked him if he was the king if the Jews. Jesus answered him: 'You said it.' Well, I say this too. Is there a crime for any man to say he is the king of the Jews; especially if he really is? When Jesus admitted he was the king of the Jews he was telling the truth and by saying this he wasn't saying he was God. Jesus was praying often and intensively his Father in heaven and always in private. It is written he was retrieving himself to do so just like he asked us to do. No one has to be God to be the king of the Jews." "I don't understand this." "Who was King David?" "He was the king of Israel, the king of the Jews." "Was he God for this much?" "No but." "There is no but. King David was the king of the Jews. Now, what did King David need to be to become the king of Israel?" "I don't really know." "I am going to refresh your memory. First he had to be <u>chosen</u> by God and also be <u>anointed</u> by God." "Now I remember; this is true." "This is true and this was true for Jesus too. Jesus was a Jew born from Mary and Joseph, who were both direct descendants of King David, which was another need to become king of the Jews. You can get the proof Jesus was chosen by God in Isaiah 53, 11. 'By his knowledge my righteous <u>servant</u> will justify many.'

See also Matthew 12, 18. 'Behold, my servant whom I have <u>chosen</u>; my beloved in whom my soul is well-pleased; I will put my Spirit on him, and he shall proclaim justice to the nations.'

Of course the Romans weren't happy about it at all and they were afraid that such a gathering king like Jesus was, a king who could resurrect the dead and heal the sick. A king who could lift up his people against this invading and dominating empire that Rome was. Can you imaging going to war against such a king; a king who can heal his sick people and resurrect his dead as soon as they fall? It would actually be impossible to eliminate such a people." "How come I never heard anyone talk about this before?" "Today there are very few Jesus' disciples who speak up like I do, if there are. This is about to change very quickly though. Babylon the great is about to fall. This was prophesied by one of God's prophets and what God said will happen; you can be sure of it.

But Jesus, the king of the Jews is not the same Jesus in all the four gospels." "What are you telling me there; this can't be, it is basically impossible." "Go read in Matthew 27, 11, in Mark 15, 2, in Luke 23, 3 and in John 18, 33-34." "Will you give me a few minutes?" "Of course I will. I will take five minutes off and get myself a cold glass of water. Would you like to have one too?" "Please, thank you." "Did you see the difference?" "It is basically the same in Matthew, Mark and Luke, but the Jesus who is in John has a lot to say for someone who was not supposed to open his mouth."

CHAPTER 9

I am on the verge to reveal myself to the world population."
"How would you do this?" "I will begin with a press conference
and I sure would like you can participate to it." "But we just
can't get a press conference just like that; we kind of have to
make the news of the day for the journalists to be interested in
it." "Believe me, they will be. I will not only make the news of
the day, but the news of the millennium." "What are you going
to invent for this to happen?" "I will invent nothing at all, but I
will arouse the curiosity of a few good journalists. Follow me and
you will see." "I wouldn't miss this for all the gold of the world."
"There you are; you too now are welling to give everything for
the kingdom of heaven, all the gold of the world." "You're funny.
You still didn't tell me what you're going to do." "I will tell a few
journalists that I follow the God of Israel and I follow Jesus of
Nazareth, the king of the Jews. Now, this will happen in Quebec
and in French, which translate like this. 'I am the God of Israel
and I am Jesus of Nazareth, the king of the Jews.'

For sure they will come to see if I am really crazy or if I can
make them a few miracles." "What will you do then?" "You will
get your answers at the press conference. Don't miss it." "I can
only say one thing; you like intrigues. Don't you think it is a bit
risky?" "It is very risky, but I count on you to continue my work
if something bad happened to me. I will choose the appropriate
time to do it and also see to get the necessary protection as well."
"They will tell you: 'If you are God, why then so much mistrust
and fear?'" "I will tell them then this is what they said to Jesus.

See Matthew 27, 35-43. "He saved others" they said, "but he can't save himself."

Jesus was crucified even though he was the King of the Jews. Rome had no respect for the kings of the Jews in those days and it is no better nowadays. Although I believe the nation of Israel is more powerful today than the nation of Italy. Do you know who had the most interest in eliminating the king of the Jews in Jesus' time?" "If I base myself on what you already said, this is got to be the Romans, the religions." "You began to shine my friend. There are huge risks that the same thing happens to me just because I follow him." "Are you sure you want to go through this?" "God gave me a job to do and I know I have to do it no matter what. The rest is in God's hands. It is up to God if he wants to come and get me before the day of the harvest and this is alright too, because the good seed is in good soil with you." "But I am not ready for this. I don't have all the answers like you do." "All the Jesus' disciples weren't ready either, but the truth made it up to us anyway. This will come for you as well; don't you worry and I'm not gone just yet." "I know this, but we can anticipate it, don't we?" "If you don't mind; I prefer you anticipate something else than my death. Be positive; be confident, God is with us." "Yes, He was with Jesus too." "Yes, He was and He is with Jesus, He is with me and He is with you, so don't worry and don't fear, just be shrewd. See what Jesus said in Matthew 28, 20. 'And surely I am with you always, to the very end of the age.'

Jesus didn't lie; the word of God is still with us, with all his disciples. Everyone who is looking for his teaching today can find it and they will always be able to find it no matter where they are. See Matthew 7, 7. 'Ask and it will be given to you; seek and you will find; knock and the door will be opened to you.'

One of the main reasons why most of the Christians didn't get Jesus' messages it is because nine and a half times out of ten and even maybe more their priests and their pastors are preaching Paul and Paul preaches Paul, not Jesus. The result of this is the Christians know Paul and his teaching, but they don't know God. All they really know about Jesus is the big lie that Jesus died on the cross for their sins and another bunch of lies and some falsified parts of the truth.

Paul was calling his disciples; 'My son.' Just like you can see it in Timothy 1, 18. 'Timothy, my son, I give you this instruction.'

See 1 Corinthians 4, 14-17. Paul wrote: 'I am not writing this to shame you, but to warn you, as my dear children. Even though you have ten thousand guardians in Christ, you do not have many fathers, for in Christ Jesus (instead of Jesus Christ) I became your father through the gospel. Therefore I urge you to imitate me. For this reason I am sending to you Timothy, my son whom I love, who is faithful in the Lord. He will remind you of my way of life in Christ Jesus, which agrees with what I teach everywhere in every church.'

Jesus told his disciples they only have one Father and He is in heaven. Jesus asked his disciples to be perfect like the heavenly Father is perfect. Jesus' way and Jesus' teaching was about his Father in heaven. Paul's teaching was about Paul and everyone of his churches.

Jesus built only one church. Do you still wonder where the hierarchy of the Christian churches is coming from? Not from Jesus and not from God, but from Paul, whom I think is the devil.

Do I have to remind you what is written in Matthew 23, 9. 'And do not call anyone on earth 'father,' for you have one Father and He is in heaven.'

This is certainly not Paul for the Jesus' disciples anyway. People who follow Jesus and do the will of God don't call anyone; 'My son.' other than their own children and they don't call anyone on earth, 'father or pastor,' other than their own biological father. All the others are antichrists and they are following the antichrist.

We already know that the devil is the king of false pride. Paul said in his statement that even ten thousand guardians in Christ are not worth the father that he is. This is a lot of modesty, don't you think?

This is almost enough to make me bringing up. We already know the devil is a big imitator and he would go as far as saying he is God. God, who said talking about his servant and to me this is Jesus. See Psalm 2, 7. '<u>I will</u> proclaim the decree of the Lord: He said to me, "You are my son; today I have become your Father.'

There are many antichrist messages in Corinthians; I'd say there is one in just about every verse. Lies and contradictions that contradict Jesus' messages are succeeding line after line. See 1 Corinthians 4, 16. 'Therefore I urge you to imitate me.'

And unfortunately so many people did it. See Matthew 5, 48 what Jesus rather said. 'Therefore, be perfect as your heavenly Father is perfect.'

See Corinthians 4, 17. 'I teach everywhere in <u>every church</u>.'

See now Jesus in Matthew 16, 18. 'I will build <u>my church</u> and the gates of Hades will not overpower it.'

'My church.' One church, so this means the one who has many churches is not Jesus and is not with Jesus either.

The leaders of these churches have imitated Paul and they have listened to Paul, but they didn't listen to Jesus at all. Paul who claimed to be a saint, who had nothing bothering his conscience and who fathered many children without touching a woman; I think he is the exact description of Satan who was thrown out of heaven with his following angels. This is not surprising then that his successors make themselves be called holy fathers in Rome, fathers in every church and other titles.

Paul didn't ask to remember the ways of Jesus, but the ways of Paul. This is what the leaders of the Christians churches did and still do. This is why Paul's ways are known and followed and Jesus' messages are ignored.

Either they are priests, fathers, holy fathers, pastors, ministers or others, they preach Paul, if not they wouldn't have built multimillion dollars properties all over the world to fill their cash registers.

I'll show you now where and when Jesus became the son of God as it was prophesied in Psalm 2, 7. 'I will proclaim the decree of the Lord: He said to me, "You are my son; today I have become your Father.'

This is the day, not before and not later.

This takes us to Jesus baptism, the day Jesus became the son of God." "Why are you saying Jesus became the son of God that day?" "Because this is the day God declared it. For Jesus to become a genuine son of God he had to do what we all have to do and this is to leave everything behind or aside to do only the will of God. This is what Jesus did.

See again Jesus in Matthew 3, 17. 'This is my Son, whom I love; with him I am well pleased.'

Did you recognize Paul's imitation? Let me bring it back for you. It is in 1 Corinthians 4, 17. 'For this reason I am sending to you Timothy, my son whom I love.'

Before that day God called Jesus his servant. This brings us to Matthew 12, 18-21. 'Behold, my servant whom I have chosen; my beloved in whom my soul is well-pleased; I will put my Spirit on him, and he shall (future) proclaim justice to the nations. He will not quarrel or cry out; (so, it is not Jesus who got upset and chased the vendors from the temple) no one will hear his voice in the streets. A bruised reed he will not break, and a smoldering wick he will not snuff out, till he leads justice to victory. In his name the nations will put their hope.'

Do you really believe God would have talked like this about Himself? I don't. All this is very near and about to happen but it is not here just yet. There are yet way too many injustices in the world to say that everything is accomplished. All the nations still need to hear what Jesus has to say and they still hope in his justice. Matthew revealed to us things we don't see anywhere else. Jesus is not dead like you were told. He said it himself that he will be resurrected. See Matthew 16, 28. 'I tell you the truth, some who are standing here will not taste death before they see the Son of Man coming in his kingdom.'

There you are; Jesus has resurrected and he came in his reign, in his kingdom, which is the kingdom of heaven. This also happened at the time some of his disciples were still alive; which means at the time of Jesus' apostles. We don't have to die to enter the kingdom of heaven, but to come out of the world. I can see the kingdom of heaven and many of Jesus' disciples saw it too before they died. This is also why Jesus said his kingdom was not of this world. This didn't mean it was an extraterrestrial kingdom for aliens.

We can see in Matthew 4, 8-9 that the world is the kingdom of the devil. We can also see that this kingdom was offered to Jesus for a price and Jesus said: "Thanks, but no thanks."

'Again, the devil took him (Jesus) to a very high mountain and showed him all the kingdoms of the world and their splendour. "All this I will give you." He said, "If you will bow down and worship me." '

The kingdom of God, the kingdom of heaven, which is Jesus' kingdom and the kingdom of the devil, which is the world, are three different kingdoms." "But all you are saying here is something never heard of before." "Almost everything! Jesus did a lot for you and me and everybody to know the whole truth, but the truth was hidden by those who were supposed or pretended to tell us the truth. They are numerous the hell angels who disguise themselves as angels of light. Just about everything I know is coming from God through the voice of Jesus." "What would happen if you go talk to priests or to pastors about those things?" "First they would tell all the members of their congregation not to talk to me anymore, because to them I am very dangerous and then they would do everything in their power to eliminate me, make me disappear. They have already tried." "You are still here and alive." "Yes, but I had to move away to survive. In the pass they have always made people like me, people who say the similar things look like crazy. This is what they did with Louis Riel who was locked up in St-Jean de Dieu, an asylum in east Montreal. On a pretence to protect him he was kept as a prisoner for almost three years by one of his supposedly friend, a bishop.

This in my opinion is the worst kind of dirt there is, I mean this bishop. Louis Riel saw the same thing I did and he talked to the wrong people about it; to priests, bishops and archbishops and they managed to get rid of him. There you are, now you are a warned man, now you know who are yours and God's enemies." "You have better luck than Louis Riel had." "Yes, so far anyway. When Louis Riel knew it, it was just too late for him, he was trapped, but he wrote things while he was in prison before he died hanged on the gallows. Just before he died he screamed; "Deliver us from evil."

He had just understood by then. Sooner or later the truth is known." "Where did you get all of this information?" "I translated a book from English to French for a Métis in Kelowna who knew a lot about the life and the career of Louis Riel. This man though didn't seem to know or understood that Louis Riel was a Jesus' disciples. I even wonder if Louis knew it. I know he knew he was a prophet of the new age, because he was saying so.

This man, this Métis is asking the Canadian Federal Government to give its pardon to Louis Riel, but this is as useless as asking Rome to give its pardon to Jesus. To receive a pardon means you are guilty, but neither Jesus nor Louis Riel was guilty. I actually made a song for Louis Riel called; He Was Only a Man.

I just showed you again, I just gave you the proof that talking to the wrong people about the word of God could be very dangerous. The history tells us a lot about it too.

You know, the inquisitions, the crusades, the supposedly witches burned alive, the wars; especially the one from 1939 to 1945 financed in part by Rome and so many other sordid crimes known and unknown from the population, not to mention the war against Israel by Rome in the years 67 to 73, where one and a half million Jews died. There are millions crimes that were committed in the name of Christianity. Jesus said the devil was a murderer from the beginning. See Matthew 23, 35. 'And so upon you will come all the righteous blood that has been shed on earth, from the blood of the righteous Abel to the blood of Zechariah, son of Berekiah, whom you murdered between the temple and the altar.'

I sometime wonder why so many people are insisting to say they are Christians. Did you ever think about reading this word starting by the end? See what this gives you: 'An-ti-christ.' This should give you something to think about. The very worst is it is true and I have all the necessary proofs to back me up." "How could you find such a thing?" "God is showing me these things and I don't even have to look for them." "This is very interesting. In one way I can't wait for your press conference and on the other way I wish you'll never go through with it." "What do you mean?" "Well, I can't wait to see people reaction, but I fear for your life." "Don't fear, nothing will happen to me if the Lord didn't allowed it and if God allows it, who are we to stop Him?" "I just know I still have a lot to learn from you." "You are on the right track now, you got the gold vein, so don't fear; it will lead you to God no matter what happened to me. You still didn't tell me your name?" "No one calls me; I am there when I need to be and when you need to talk to me." "Now you are the one who is intriguing me. Who are you?" "I told you all you need to know about me for now." "Will you come back to pursue this conversation?" "I have a lot to swallow, a lot to digest for now, but as I told you; I still have a lot to learn from you. I will come back when I feel capable to take some more." "Thanks for listening to me." "All of the pleasure was for me. Shalom!

I kept writing in this book wondering if I was ever going to hear from him again. He really said he will come back if he needs it. I must say that I miss him a lot. He seems to be asking all the questions the average people would ask.

Then the days went by and the day of the press conference was approaching rapidly. I knew very well I was going to risk my life by exposing myself this way to the population as well as my identity. I also knew this was an extraordinary and special occasion to make Jesus' messages, the word of God known to people. I also know the day all the nations know the truth the end will be at the door.

At this time all the people of all the nations of the world will understand Jesus' messages, the word of God. People who will accept it will be saved. They will not be all saved from the tortures by the beast, by the religious and governmental system, but they will be saved from the flames of hell.

See Matthew 10, 28. 'Do not be afraid of those who kill the body, but can't kill the soul. Rather, be afraid of the One who can destroy both soul and body in hell.'

If you don't believe in tortures, just go read about the stories of the inquisitions and about the crusades and the supposed witches burnt alive, the story more recent of Louis Riel without forgetting the last world war with Hitler supported by Rome and its demons. All of these crimes done by the clergy and do not think this is only things of the pass.

The love of the most has already cooled off today more than it ever was. The power of the holy people is about to be broken like it is prophesied in Daniel 12, 7.

I can understand that God doesn't accept to loose after all He has done to save the world. After sending so many prophets to tell us what to do, how to be and so on and see half of his creation choosing the devil and hell, this would be enough to inflame his anger. Yet all God was asking us to do through Jesus, his son and servant was to repent to be free from the slavery of sin.

Don't forget that Jesus only save the ones who listen to this message, put it in practice and it is just for this reason he said it.

Today I started another hymn for my Lord and it's called: You Chose Me Lord.

You chose me Lord to speak to sinners
You chose me Lord, is it a curse?
You gave me the words for my songs
To tell to nations where there're wrong
Jesus too knew he was going to die

He did what he had to for the Most High
Like Jesus did it too, I'll do your will
Is it my destiny to die on the hill?

So after writing this song I went out to cut the grass and guess who was waiting out there for me walking back and forth along the road and waiting for the right moment to talk to me. This was my no name friend. It was just a beautiful evening and there was a gentle breeze just enough to keep mosquitoes away. This was an early Friday evening just before the Sabbath was about to begin. I always do my very best to do all of my work in the six days the Lord allows me to do it. This is just a normal thing to do; I mean to please our Father when we love Him with all of our heart. Then I stopped my riding lawnmower to salute him.

"Hi there, my no name friend." "Hi to you too, my spiritual guide. James, I was wondering when and if you could give me more tips on how to become a disciple." "You mean a Jesus' disciple?" "Yes, yes, that's it." "Well, tomorrow would be for me the right time." "Tomorrow is the Sabbath day, isn't it wrong to work on that day?" "It is never wrong to do something good on that day; either it is to pull a sheep out of the pit or to help another one reaching the kingdom of heaven. Besides, helping you understanding the will of God is not at all a job to me and neither a work to help me making a living." "This is well said." "Jesus was going in the temple and in the synagogues on Saturday, the last day of the week to preach, because this was the day where the Jews got together over there, which is still their day, he who wanted to gather together all the lost sheep of Israel." "There is another thing which is buggering me about the Sabbath and what Jesus would have done on that day." "And what this is?" "This is the fact he would have cursed a fruit tree, a fig tree that had nothing to offer him when he was hungry." "Do you really believe Jesus would have cursed a man who was too poor to give him anything?" "No, not at all!" "Me neither." "So, how do you explain this statement?" "This is very personal, but this reminds me of Paul who wants to make people believe faith is more important than deeds by getting salvation by faith through grace." "So you think this is weeds planted in Matthew's garden?" "It sure looks like it. I also believe there are a lot less weeds in Matthew than in the other gospels, but still, there are some." "I don't recall seeing them; you're intriguing me again." "I will talk to you about it tomorrow, unless you help me now and come to my house after my work is done. For now I have to finish this before the sundown, because then the Sabbath will begin and the grass will be too long and hard to cut next week." "You really have at heart this commandment?" "I love my God with all of my heart and my love is so little compare to his." "How this love for the Lord came to you?" "I think in the bottom of my heart this love has always been there, but the more I learnt to know Him, the more I learnt to love Him. I think the same thing happened to Jesus and this is the reason he went as far as given his live to fulfill his mission. This didn't make him suicidal, but rather a man with a lot of courage." "Put it this way, it makes sense." "It is the only way to look at it, because this is the true story. God didn't sacrificed Jesus on the cross more than He sacrificed Isaac on a stake. God said it Himself that he doesn't take any pleasure with sacrifices. Take a look at Samuel 15, 22. 'Does the Lord delight in burnt offerings and sacrifices as much as obeying the voice of the Lord? To obey is better than sacrifice, and heed is better than the fat of rams.'

To obey God's word is also better than to say the abomination which is found in John 1, 29. 'Behold, the lamb of God who takes away the sin of the world!'

They are simple enough and easy to understand these words." "But you have to finish your work before it's too late." "This is right too. We'll continue this conversation inside if you want to. I can be done within ten minutes."

Then I finished my work that seemed endless contrary to the usual.

It is amazing how talking about the word of God is getting me passionate.

We both came to the house after putting the equipment in the shed. Then I offered a cold glass of water to my no name friend and I took one for myself too.

"You were talking about the sacrifice which you say God is not found of and you also say God didn't sacrificed his Son." "God cursed the country of Canaan because they were sacrificing there first born, saying this were some abominations, do you really believe He could have done the same thing?" "This in fact would make no sense at all, you're right." "You said it. Take a look in Isaiah 1, 11." "'The multitudes of your sacrifices—what are they to me?' Says the Lord. "I have more than enough of burnt offerings, of <u>rams</u> and the fat of fattened animals; I have no pleasure in the blood of bulls and <u>lambs</u> and goats.""

This is clear enough too." "You said it. I am sure also that God didn't have any pleasure in the murder of his beloved Son. Take a look also in Isaiah 66, 3. 'But whoever sacrifices a bull is like one who kills a man, and whoever <u>offers a lamb,</u> ('the lamb of God who takes away the sin of the world.') is like one who breaks a dog's neck; whoever makes a grain offering is like one who presents pig's blood, and whoever <u>burns memorial incense</u> is like one who worships an idol. They have chosen their own ways, and their souls delight in their <u>abominations</u>.'

God said the one who sacrifices a lamb is committing an abomination and He would have done it?????? Please think again, would you?

Many leaders of the churches nowadays are still offering their sacrifices of the mass and are still burning some incense at their Sunday's morning services. They are still offering these abominations and they are still taking pleasure in doing so. All this on the first day of the week, on Sunday, the day of the sun. This confirms by the same token that they don't have the same God I have, the God of Israel. They have for god the god of Rome, which I think is Satan. Again the first day is contrary to the last day.

Now, let's just be clear here. We can read in John 3, 16. 'For God so loved the world that <u>He gave his one and only Son,</u>

(which means He sacrificed his son) that whoever believes in him (like demons do) shall not perish but have eternal life.'

(This is an action God himself said was an abomination)

This guy, this John also said that God so loved the world and God asked us through Jesus to retrieve from the world, because it is the kingdom of the devil. God almost destroyed this world with the flood because of its abominations.

This brings me to another song I made and it's called: The Before Noon Sundays.

They lied to me, they cheated me every Sunday morning. They lied to me, they cheated me, that's why I like to sing. The Lord told me the Sabbath day is Saturday, but the Sunday who is it for? Is there another lord? They lied to me, they cheated me......."

"You don't mince your words." "Jesus too said what ever he had to say and he is my model." "I can see that, but it is very risky." "Everything I say is very risky no matter how I say it, mind as well be frank and direct. They fear the power of Jesus for a long time; otherwise they would have killed him a lot sooner. There is another important message from Jesus about sacrifices I want to show you and it is in Matthew 9, 13. 'But go and learn what this means: I desire mercy, not sacrifice.' For I have not come to call the righteous, but sinners.'

This also means there were some righteous people even at the Jesus time.

Jesus wanted to warn some sinners who wanted to get out of their slavery, some blinds who wanted to see the truth, some lost sheep who wanted to reach the rest of the flock and God, their pastor."

"I see that you are writing on your computer, aren't you afraid to get your book stolen?" "If a thief wants to die instead of me, let him do so; as long as the messages are getting on the market." "This is a very good way to see things."

"So, I was saying that the leaders of some churches are still offering some sacrifices to God who doesn't desire them. I would say that the closer you are to a religion the farther you are from

God, because then you are under the devil charming ways. Although, Jesus did a lot to warn us and to get us out of the devil's trap. I might even be your last chance, because I preach Jesus' messages and at this point in time I don't know anyone else who is doing this." "You look tired; you most likely had a long week. If you don't mind we can continue this conversation tomorrow." "This will be alright too. Do you have a long way to find a bed for the night? If so you are welcome to stay here for the night, because I have a spare bedroom." "No, I have a place near by." "You're not talking about a place under the stars? Don't be shy; you are welcome even if I don't know your name." "How could you trust me to this point? Maybe I want to still your book." "Are you ready to die instead of me? We cannot steal our way to God, we have to deserve it. Would you like something to eat before going to bed?" "No, I'm find thank you." "I'll see you in the morning then for breakfast. Good night!" "Have a good night too. Ho James, it's good to listen to you." "Thanks! Would you tell me your name some day?" "I _am_ here." "See you in the morning.

I was tired and even so I had a hard time to go to sleep. The only fact my guest didn't want to tell me his name was bothering me. When I was half way between being asleep and awake a few hours later my cat came near my shoulder. He who is not allowed to come above my knee. This was just for a second or two, but this was long enough for him to let go one of the worst bugs we have around here. The wood tick bothered me more than the fact the cat disobeyed me. I felt it run all over my back right away and then I turned around and I robbed my back against the bed sheet trying to get rid of it. Then I turned on the lamp, put my glasses on to see this little harmful bug trying to get away. I grabbed it quickly and put it where it could hurt no one anymore. Those are a very bad nuisance around here. When they reach the spot on your body they feel it's right they put their head through your skin and suck your blood just like a vampire if you give them time. They are small, let's say just one eight of an inch in diameter, but they can quickly reach one inch with your blood. I found one on the floor one time that fell off my dog that was the size of a big marble. I got bitten three years ago by one of those, right under my shoulder blade and I had to take a long knife to take it off with the help of a few mirrors. I was bled, it was quite painful and it took three weeks to heal. It is not always easy to live alone. Most of the time when you're awake you can feel it and get rid of it before getting hurt. They usually cause a kind of an itch you should not neglect when you know they are around. They say their bites can cause a person to be temporarily paralysed and also lime disease. They can also kill animals; especially the deer when they are enough of them. I collect a lot of them after I have petted one of my dogs. Buster, my oldest dog had a lot of them on him after we came back from fishing, because they are always there by the thousands in high grass near the water. This said; it was not easy at all for me to go back to sleep after. My animals would never know to which point I am protecting them, but without knowing this they have for me an unconditional love.

I hope my no name friend had better luck than me for a good night sleep. I would have like to have a few hours more to sleep this morning, but good manners kind of forced me to get up and get the breakfast ready for my guest and for myself.

I have to keep my mouth shut about these bugs too; otherwise he might just be afraid to come back as much as my mom did. It is near eight o'clock and the tea flavour will most likely wake him up. This is exactly what happened.

"Hi you." "Good day! How are you this morning?" "I had better nights but I'll be fine." "Does your book bother your sleep?" "No, not at all, but I admit it, it is a lot on my mind." "I myself had a very good sleep. I'd say more; I can say that I slept like an angel. I can tell you though that I am very intrigued about what you said concerning the weeds in the gospel of Matthew. I have never seen in there something that doesn't seem normal." "I will talk to you about it after breakfast. What would you like to eat?" "One egg and bacon would be fine for me with a good cup of tea. It smells so good." "I am sorry, but you will not find pork meat in my house." "It's true, you don't eat pork." "You should make it a habit too; if you want to say that the God of Israel is your God. We cannot mock Him unpunished forever, you should know this." "I was forgetting, but you're right, it is important to do his will." "Millions of people are praying God saying: 'Your will be done on earth as it is in heaven.' But they are neglecting his will completely." "Now that you mentioned it I realized that it is very true. People are saying the Lord's prayer and in this prayer it is mentioned the will of God; the same God who doesn't want his children to eat pork and millions are eating pork bacon just about every day with their breakfast." "Of course it is the will of God that we don't eat meat or anything that is not proper for our body." "Isn't it written in the Acts of the apostles that what God has made clean is pure?" "We have to pay attention to where this is coming from. The Acts of the apostles, which I call the Acts of Paul at 95% or more were written by Luke, Paul's love one. In fact this was the first clue that put me on the antichrist trail." "What is it?" "The fact that most of the Acts speak about Paul and that Paul preaches and contradicted Jesus' messages in just about everything.

Now getting back to Peter and what is pure and impure to eat; Peter will tell you himself this never happened and this was invented so the pig's breeders can sell more of their meat. Peter has never spoke against God's will in his entire life, I'm sure of it. What ever God called impure like mice, rats and pigs will stay impure forever. This was just another cunning trick from the crafty one to trap people. By seeing what is happening today we can almost say that he succeeded; especially with the pagans directed by Paul and company." "I thought Luke was a good apostle." "You will find out as you read too that he is another crafty one, another devil disguised as an angel of light." "Do you have at least another proof to say such a thing?" "I actually have something which is very obvious. But I will let you find it by yourself. Read and compare the genealogy of Jesus in Luke with the genealogy of Jesus in Matthew. You will find out that they are different from one another." "But this is impossible.

There is only one Jesus' possible and real genealogy." "You said it, but they are different from one place to the other." "So one or the other is a liar." "You said it and I am persuaded this is not Matthew and besides, I got the proof and I know the reason why the change was made." "I never heard about this before." "Talk to me again when you found out and be very careful when you read" "I will, I promise." "If you want to read I'll let you have my Bible. I have to leave for an hour to go feed my dogs and just let's hope you have it found by the time I'm back." "You're not afraid to leave me alone in your house?" "You're not alone; my God is looking after me and on what ever belongs to me. He wouldn't allow me to leave a thief alone with my goods and in my house. See you in a bit." "See you."

One hour later!

How are they?" "They are fine. They are always happy to see me. They sure are my best friends on earth. It is a bit sad to say this, but it's true. This is not something I would do, but even if I would kick them they would turn around and come to leak my hand. I have seen once a very bad master, completely loveless for his dog and he was loved by it. It might even have been the only creature on earth who loved him.

Did you find what we were talking about?" "No, I read both twice and I was reading this for the third time and I can't tell you where the difference is." "And yet, it is there. You do agree with me that only one genealogy for one person is possible?" "I agree with you that each one of us can only have one true family tree. I will never be the ancestral of my cousins and neither of any of their children." "I will show you now where the lie is. I was going to say the mistake, but this was no mistake, it was done deliberately. They have deliberately eliminated a great figure in Luke for a simple and unique reason that I will tell you after you see what this is all about. Not only they eliminated him, but they have also replaced him by his brother." "You are the more and more intriguing, but this would be a very heavy swindle." "Just wait, you'll see. Take the Bible at the beginning of Matthew. What can you read?" "Let me see. 'Genealogy of

Jesus. A record of the genealogy of Jesus Christ <u>the son of David</u>, the son of Abraham.'

This is not a lie. Jesus was really a descendant of David and David a descendant of Abraham." "This is not what I was talking about, but just remember this anyway, that Jesus is the son of David. This will be important for another answer a little bit farther." "Ok!" "Now go read to see who inherited the throne of David in Matthew." "Let see, this is Matthew 1, 6. 'David was the father of Solomon, whose mother had been Uriah's wife.'

I always knew this." "What you didn't seem to know is the fact that the son of David in Luke is not Solomon." "Come on now, this is impossible." "Go read now who is the son of David in Luke." "Let see, this is Luke 3, 31. 'The son of Nathan, the son of David.'

Well, how could they make such a mistake?" "I told you; this was not a mistake. They deliberately made the change of the history." "How will you explain this one to me?" "It's actually very simple. Paul didn't like women and neither did Luke. Do you see? Solomon had just too many wives and concubines for the good pleasure of these two and for the popes, the cardinals, the bishops and priests; so they just took him off the history. They probably thought no one will ever see it; so they were please with their lie. No one ever mentioned it to me either." "That's a good one. But I could have read these two gospels a hundred times without seeing the difference. I did it and thousands of others did too. But how can you explain why you saw the difference?" "I told you before; God showed me how to write and how to read too and especially how to pay attention of what I am reading." "But this morning I was being very careful to what I was reading and not only this; I was also looking specifically for the difference." "God was not ready to show it to you before I do. He certainly wanted to give me a chance to do it. There are many people to whom I spoke about it and none of them so far could show me where the difference is. Some of them told me they saw it, but they couldn't tell me where it is, which simply means they never saw it. Years ago when someone saw things like that they went to the church and told their priest about it and the result of this was that a few changes were made in the Bible." "Do you have another example for me?" "I sure do. One is in John 13, 4. Do you want to read it yourself?" "I wouldn't mind this. 'So Jesus got up from the meal, <u>took off his outer clothing</u>, and wrapped a towel around his waist.' "

"See now how it is written in an older Bible, I mean the original. Read again, will you?" "Of course I will. 'Jesus got up from supper and laid aside his garments; and taking a towel, he girded himself.'

But this doesn't make sense at all; he had only two pieces of clothing. The son of God, who some people say he is God would have got naked in front of his disciples in those days. I am sure that any descent man wouldn't have done this." "For this John, the John of this gospel it was supper time. Now if this Jesus took a towel to gird himself; this is because he was naked. Do you see what I mean now? In the newer Bibles, like the international Jesus took off his <u>outer clothing</u> before washing the feet of his apostles, but when he was done, he put on <u>his clothes</u>. Read it for yourself in John 13, 12. 'When Jesus had finished washing their feet, he put on his clothes and returned to his place.' "

"This means that Jesus would have taken his long robe off before and put on a robe and an underwear after. I see; they were smart enough to change the story in one place, but not in the other. They were cheaters but not very brilliant. Talking about brilliant, you got to be so to find all this." "Jesus mentioned it in the parable of the weeds." "Come on now; I have never seen this either." "Just read Matthew 13, 43." "'Then the righteous will shine like the sun in the kingdom of their Father.'

You're right again." "They are caught in their lies today and I don't think they really know how to get out of it. The truth will put them down and they know it. The sword will hit and the beast will be hurt. The great Babylon will fall. It is written that it will fall in one hour. This is about the time it takes for a news to make it all around the world nowadays." "You're right; with all the satellites they have today it is not very long for news to go around the world. But how the ancient prophets could know these things and tell others like thousands of years ahead of time like Daniel did it?" "God was telling them the same way He is talking to me today. Some of them knew how to listen too and there is no reason for God not to talk to us today." "I have to agree with you; you sure know and see things others didn't see and still don't see." "I even knew how to find Ben Laden long before they caught him, but the FBI didn't want to listen to me. I won't say more about this though.

I asked a pastor from a Baptist church once what he thinks about Solomon and his answer was: 'Not much.'

Solomon was most likely the wisest king ever to live on this earth beside Jesus and this man doesn't think much about him. Solomon did more for his country, for Israel with his wives and concubines than all the other kings combined with all of their wars." "Is this possible?

You mentioned before there were some contradictions in Matthew also, could you show me them?" "Sure, it will be my pleasure. Do you remember the beginning of Matthew?" "I can go back to it. 'Genealogy of Jesus. A record of the genealogy of Jesus Christ <u>the son of David</u>, the son of Abraham.' "

"I told you that this was the truth." "I know this is the truth, because Jesus has to be a direct descendant of King David to be the King of the Jews, the king of Israel, the Christ, the Messiah like many prophets have predicted. But?" "But in Matthew 22, 41-46, Jesus would have denied being the son of David when many other times he let people called him son of David without denying it; like it is written in Matthew 21, 15. "Hosanna to the son of David."

There are three contradictions in Matthew 22, 41-46. 'While the Pharisees were gathered together, <u>Jesus</u> asked them: "What do you think about the Christ? Whose son is he?" "The son of David," they replied. He said to them, "How is it then that David, speaking by the Spirit, calls him 'Lord'? For he says, "'The Lord said to my Lord: "Sit at my right hand until I put your enemies under your feet." ' If then David calls him 'Lord' how can he be his son?" No one could say a word in reply, and from that day on no one dared ask him any more questions.'

I understand no one would ask anymore questions to this impostor no matter who he is. I think this is a liar. This is Paul's style really.

First, never Jesus would have denied being the son of David, because for one thing if he is not the son of David he cannot be the Christ. The second contradiction in this story is that the Pharisees are telling the truth while this Jesus is lying" "This doesn't make any sense either." "Right!" "I don't see anything else even by looking very carefully." "No one dared asking him anymore questions while it was this Jesus who was asking questions to the Pharisees." "James, you are incredible." "You're impressed?" "You bet that I am." "I only hope this book will open the eyes of many people and these people would turn to God instead of looking for god in some churches where the true God doesn't want to be in. But I am afraid many will turn against God for thinking God left them in the dark. In 99 per cent of the time if they are in the dark it is because they didn't want to see the truth." "How do you know God doesn't want to be in churches?" "It is written God doesn't enter a box made by men's hands. Take a look in Isaiah 66, 1. 'This is what the Lord says: "Heaven is my throne, and the earth is my footstool. Where is the house you will build for Me? Where will my <u>resting</u> place be?" '

This is another proof God didn't take is day of rest yet.

God lives in the heart of the righteous people; there is where God's temple is. God protects his children and in my case I can say He speaks to me and I listen. I love Him and He loves me thousands of times more." "I spent a marvellous time with you James and I hope we can do this again another time, but you said there was some other contradictions in Matthew, can you tell me what it is?" "Of course I can. Look in Matthew 12, 31-32. 'And so I tell you, every sin and blasphemy will be forgiven men, but anyone who speaks against the Spirit will not be forgiven. Anyone who speaks against the Son of Man will be forgiven, but anyone who speaks against the Holy Spirit (against Paul, see John 14, 26) will not be forgiven, either in this age or in the age to come.'

Jesus didn't condemn anyone and this message condemns. For one thing all the sins are against God; so they are against his Spirit too. This message is from Paul, I could bet my life on this. Paul who pretended he is the spirit to come, the Counselor. Paul can see everything without being there. See Colossians 2, 5. 'For though I am absent from you in body, I am with you in <u>spirit</u> and delight <u>to see</u> how orderly you are and how firm your faith in Christ is.'

This is not a small thing." "I don't see anything wrong in what he's saying." "You don't see that he's telling his disciples, his followers that he can see them no matter what they're doing; even if he is not with them in person and pretending to be God and the spirit. I am telling you this is devilish and it is him or one of his disciples who wrote Matthew 12, 31-32. I am telling you too that Matthew didn't write this and Jesus never said what is there either. Jesus asked his Father to forgive the ones who were killing him and here he would condemn someone for a blasphemy. It doesn't make any sense at all." "You're right, but why are you getting so upset?" "Do you realize how many people could have thought they had no chance at all to be saved and with this thought turned away from God? How many do you think felt condemned without even having a chance to be forgiven, not ever and they gave up on God because of this lie, because of this liar?

To see such abomination in the Bible is enough for someone to turn on God permanently. Please go read now what it is written in 1 John 1, 9." "'If we confess our sins, He is faithful and just and will forgive us our sins and purify us from <u>all</u> unrighteousness.'

This includes the blasphemy against the real Holy Spirit. God forgives all to all who sincerely repent. This is the truth. You will see as you keep reading that Paul often condemns. This is not from God, it is not from Jesus and it is not from Matthew

JAMES PRINCE

either. God saves, the devil condemns, the word of God judges."
"But how can you say one thing is true and another one is false?"
"I told you before. Don't forget what is written in Matthew 7, 18.
'A good tree cannot bear bad fruits, and a bad tree cannot bear
good fruits.'

There was an important reason for Jesus to tell us this. When
you'll see in the Scriptures something that doesn't seem right to
you; just don't take for granted it is all true. At least search for
the truth. Take for example Psalm 83 when you have a chance
to read it; you will see that this guy has a totally different policy
than Jesus or David about forgiving. You will see as well this
guy is the only one to pronounce the name of the Lord in the
Bible. Even Jesus didn't dare doing this. This is different for the
devil and his angels though. I believe the J.….Witnesses built
their church on this Psalm to form their religion. By doing so
they make almost everyone who talks about them breaking the
second God's commandment in the face of the world and this
either they talk good or bad. They make people taking the name
of the Lord in vain, unnecessarily.

Jesus always referred to God by saying either; 'The Father in
heaven or my Father who is in heaven." "I think you just made
yourself another bunch of enemies." "Yes, maybe another billion
or so. Jesus didn't restrain himself about the truth and he wasn't
preaching to make friends, but to make to truth known to the
world no matter if they like it or not. This is most likely why he
often had to flee and why he had no place to rest his head.

Most of these Witnesses are just like the Catholics and the
Christians; they are blinds lead by blinds.

They are not all blinds though, because I know for sure that
some of the pastors know the truth, but they hide it voluntarily
to protect their business, their religion. When one of my sisters
went to talk to her pastor at her church about a few things;
I mean lies and contradictions I mentioned to her; she was
asked to leave and the other members of his church were told
not to talk to her anymore. A very similar situation happened
to me at the church I was going to in Westside Kelowna. The

only difference was that I left before they asked me to do it, but the other members of this church weren't allowed to talk to me anymore. Jesus is right when he said: 'They shut down the kingdom of heaven in people's face.'

The truth is very dangerous for the sixth biggest business in North America. It will fall anyway the Great Babylon. Like I said it. I think it is only a question of about twenty years. I know I am doing my share for this to happen no matter how high are the risks." "Well, I have to go now, but I would like to do this again another time." "You know you are welcome anytime you want, don't you?" "I thank you for your help and also for your hospitality." "This is nothing, see you soon." "Shalom!"

It's good to have someone to talk to and someone who listen. Jesus even though he had a tragic end was lucky to have someone who listened to him and us even luckier that someone did. For me even though I have a big family I don't have many among them to whom I can talk to about the word of God. Oh, if I wanted to talk to them about the lies and the contradictions they already have accepted, there will be no problem at all. I would be welcome then. It is very sad though, but Jesus and Louis Riel went through this too and Jesus told us we will go through this as well.

CHAPTER 10

It looks like no matter where I go, no matter where I move the devil sends his demons against me.

I guess it is not a bad idea for me to let you know my situation here in this village. When I moved here three years ago the mayor of this village whom I cannot name for legal reasons showed me around what was for sale and so on. This is a small village of about sixty voters. I let him know I was interested to buy some properties knowing they were kind of cheap. A man and his wife who came from the same place I'm from, which is Westbank BC, bought a very nice property here and this for a very decent price. They bought a house and a garage on a four acres piece of land for two thousand two hundred and fifty dollars. I found out about it because I am the one who moved them here. So I knew I could buy some properties here too for some good prices. So the mayor showed me what was for sale and mainly what was cheap. So I didn't waste any time to make plans for my future. There was a very big shop of forty feet wide by one hundred feet long already in demolition on a bunch of lots that totals two hundred and seventy-five feet wide by one hundred and twenty feet deep. I got the whole thing for $1500. 00. I also found a decent house of forty-eight feet by twenty-seven on one an a half acre and this for one thousand dollars. I was so short of money that it took me more than a year to pay it; so I gave him five hundred dollars in rent for compensation. It was worth it. Behind this house there are three other houses, but only one is humanly liveable, but each one of them is on a nice piece of land of one hundred and sixty feet wide by two hundred feet deep and all of them of very nice top soil. I got the three of them for one thousand dollars and with that all the time I needed to pay for them. I can't ask for more. To make a long story short I'll tell you that I own now here in this village of Goodadam Saskatchewan five houses, a large shop that I rebuilt, a store on the corner of the main street and the highway, which will become the spot for one of the largest hubcaps collection of this country with over ninety thousand pieces, a two stories hall on a four acres piece of land and seven other lots and I got all of this for less than twelve thousand dollars.

But good things rarely come with only good things. The mayor knowing I was a carpenter offered me a fifty, fifty association in his construction business and he didn't waste much time to show me what he was capable of. It was not a single day without him stopping at the liquor store to buy a big bottle and a six pack. He was locking himself every night with his drinks. One could knock at his door all he wants; he was not opening to anyone and neither answering the phone.

At seven o'clock the next morning he was at my doorstep asking for a beer as he said for good luck in the day.

After doing two or three little jobs of no importance he began to disappear for full days with no apparent valid reason. I cover the large roof of the presbytery for a Catholic church in Itunara on which I worked more than sixty hours at one hundred and five degrees and he worked less than twenty hours on it.

The only thing is he wanted to get fifty per cent of the money for it. Before we settled this last one we had started to replace the shingle on a house near the village. Everything went fine to take off the old shingles and we were four guys to do it. There was the owner of the house who was helping and he had his tractor with a big bucket to take away all the waste. There was also a friend of the mayor, the mayor and myself. Within a little more than one hour half of the roof was ready to receive the new shingles. But then the mayor said he forgot to take his compressor, his nailers and his nails with him, so he went home.

He went to get these tools which were indispensable for us to complete the work. All three of us were waiting for this man (if I can say) for two and one half hours for this guy who was gone three miles away. We asked his friend what could have happened. His response was: 'What do you think?'

No doubt there were most likely a few drops left in the bottom of his bottles.

When he came back a little before noon we started covering this roof right away, but guess what, he was doing it backward. Instead of covering form left to right he was doing it the other way. So I told him he was working backward and he seemed to be all surprised. I told him it was hard enough to work on a roof without having to do it backwardly. His friend said then that I was capable to do it too. I said no way; if he can't work properly I rather go home. Then the owner who was looking from the ground level told the mayor he was going all crooked. It was true. So I had to take over and start covering this roof normally from left to right. Luckily we only had six rows done by then. At around four in the afternoon we had this half of the roof done and everything was fine except these four first rows. I told the landlord this was not hurting the quality of the roof and he wouldn't most likely never look at this part of the roof for another twenty years. This was accepted, but he really had the intention to make the mayor fix his bad work. Everything was bad but ended well.

When the evening came my associate came to my place to settle the job done at the church. He had made his calculations at fifty, fifty. "I don't think so", I said. "This is not the way I learned to count. We are at fifty, fifty at work too. I can understand that you have to leave from time to time, but other than this you have to work too. If you want to be fair you'll pay me $15.00 an hour for my hours and do the same for the hours you worked. I allow you $150.00 more to you for getting the contract. You owe me $1225.00 and you earned $575.00. If you can't be fair I have no more business to do with you." "I'm the one who got the contract." "And you are largely paid for this too."

He grumbled a bit, he gave me my money and he went home. I was waiting for him to pick me up the next morning but he never showed up. I started to look for him three days later and I found him in Itunara, the next town, a town of around six hundred inhabitants fifteen miles West of Goodadam. I found him, but he seemed to want to hide. I went to talk to him anyway and he told me that our arrangement wasn't working for him anymore. This is perfect, I said and I went on the spot to put a little ad in the newspaper. One more time I was on my own again and this with only a few dollars.

I don't know if he realized it or not, but by setting me free he did me a great favour. I am not a quitter and it would have taken me a lot to let him down, but this way everything was fine with me.

Three weeks later the owner of the house where I worked on half of the roof came to see me and he asked me if I would go finish the other side of the roof. I was working then on my own property demolishing the rest of the shop I bought. Of course I will I said, but I thought it was done long time ago. 'No.' He said. 'I didn't see him since.' Talking about the mayor, my ex partner.

"You will get paid by the insurances." "I hope they're not going to take months to do so, because I can't afford to wait too long." "If it's too long I'll pay you myself and they can always pay me back." "If it's the case I'll do it."

Two days later I was on his roof and with his help I started to clean the second side of his roof. A couple of hours later the mayor with his drinking body came to get his tools thinking probably I was going to use them. The owner of the house I guess saw this coming and for this reason he stayed on the sight, because beside for getting his tools these guys wanted to make a number on me.

I started at eight o'clock in the morning and I finished with the sundown. All I had left to do the next day was the cap, about one and a half hour. I did the whole thing with a hammer. In fifteen hours I earned $1100.00.

I talked to the mayor about the other side of the roof I worked on and he told me to claim the whole thing from the insurance for myself. This is what I did without any remorse. I didn't waste any time to go buy myself a good compressor and a roofing air nailer. This was the last roof I have done with a hammer.

The reason why the mayor didn't go back to finish this roof was because he could not get the money from it for a long time and he needed the money every day for his drink. This is why he was in this little town carrying water for a farmer at eight dollars an hour, because this way he could get enough money every day for his bottles.

But this was not the end of his troubles and neither mine. A year later work was getting hard to get for him; so he got into his head the best thing to do for him was to hurt me and my reputation. The insurance agent told me he will never deal with him again and many costumers told me they had to wait for him up to two years the get their roof repaired. Two years is very long; especially when the roof is leaking.

So they say he was found knocked down near his house on the sidewalk with his head opened. Apparently he told the police I beat him up with the help of three other guys disguised as soldiers. This is what he tells everyone who want to listen to him as well. According to the feedback from the people I talked to, many believed him too. What is better than to put dirt on someone's reputation to get yours better? It is a method used by politicians a lot.

Lucky for me the policemen didn't believe in his story and they put him under observation instead where he still is as far as I know. His friend who was on the roof with us came to his rescue right away and called the mayor's sister in Calgary who came running to him. The idea for sure was to get help getting out of his mess that was almost impossible. This was not too bad of an idea really. In one shot he was getting me charged for assault, hurting my reputation, have his sister to pay his unpaid taxes, what would allow him to save his house and maybe many costumers would turn to him to get their roof repaired. He had just lost his job as a mayor for a fraudulent election, because seven voters who voted for him were dead and some of them for many years. There have been many other frauds in the village during his time as a mayor. Corruptions don't only happen in big towns like Montreal.

I know for example that he put liens on houses for unpaid taxes while his weren't paid for more than three years. No lien on his house, but I think it is done now with the new mayor.

A few days later while I was working in my garden planting my potatoes I heard a voice that I recognized right away. It was the voice of the ex mayor's drinking body who I thought was looking for his dog or something. He was swearing his head off and saying all kind of vulgarities like: 'Now I got you, you son of a bitch, now you're going to pay for everything you've done.'

What I didn't know at the time is he was talking about me. It was not very long before I found out what he wanted. He was drunk but he made his way up to me anyway and he asked me what I was doing there on this land. "Leave me alone," I said, "I have too much to do to waste my time with your stupidities." "What are you doing here? This land doesn't belong to you, you have no business here." "This is my garden; so leave me alone and go home; I have a lot of work to do." "You have no business here and I am going to kill you and bury you in your potatoes."

Then he got near me and he tried to hit me. I managed to avoid the hit and I gave him a good one on the mouth. He then back up a little and I found out he had a very hard head. I then tried to walk away from him, but he came at me again and knowing his head was very hard I swung around with the handle of the rake I had in my hands and I hit him right in his forehead while I aimed at his mouth.

Of course he had his head opened and he left slapping his hands, bleeding like a pig, happy as one can be and saying: 'Now I know it's you who hit my friend, now I caught the guilty party.'

Then he went to his other drinking body, the one I moved here from BC. They called the cops which I found out from the policeman who came to question me, but I had called to cops too.

He told the police officer I hit him with an axe. If this was the case he would have been dead even though he had a hard head.

The police officer came to question me and to inspect the sight where all this took place. I showed him the broken rake handle I used and we could never find the missing piece. He told me that if it wasn't for the fact this guy was very nasty with the cops and with the ambulance people he would have had to charge me with assault with a weapon. I told him that I was assaulted and I acted in self-defence. He said he can believe it considering the way the other guy acted with them.

I know for sure that in BC I would have been charged, this is guaranteed, because I know they charge innocent people over there and they let go some guilty ones.

So I sent this drunk to the hospital where he could be with his drinking companion, with his friend. the ex mayor. I think they had the chance together to make other plans to hurt me.

The next summer the same drunk came after me for revenge while I was working on one of my costumer's house in the village. At first he wanted to avenge his friend and then he wanted to avenge both of them. He came to catch me twice where many people saw him. So I called the police again and he went to hide at one of my neighbour's place. This was mainly to get someone to drive his truck back home because he has lost his driver's license long time ago. The cops went to his place to arrest him and charged him with the intention to harm someone. He told the cops I had reasons to fear him because soon or later he will get me and it was just a question of time. He tried to stop me a few more times in the street and I reported this too, but I listen to the cops who told me to stay away from them, that they were both very dangerous.

He had to appear in court a year later, but the crown attorney decided there were not enough proofs against him and they let him go free.

If I miss to stop at a stop sign I get caught and if I don't pay the fine I get pursued even more. This guy drives continually drunk without driver's license, he runs after people in the street to harm him, he threats to hurt someone and he even told the cops this, he made death threats and he gets away as if nothing happened.

What is the question? What is the answer? Where is the justice? Does someone have to be hurt for life before the justice can do something against him? What's the matter with our justice system?

As far as I am concerned, with all of the injustices that I have known, seen and heard, either they are directed against me or others; I would rename this system and I would call it: 'The court of injustices, the injustice's system.'

Is it because I am only a little man alone and French, not too rich in the West Canadian, a drop in the ocean without any importance that I could never get more than five per cent of justice? Maybe so!

I sure would like to get an answer to these questions. I even thought about sending this article to a journalist who might himself wanted to know the answer.

Three weeks ago this same man, the same drunk was chasing me in the streets in his pick up drunk as one can be and without driver's license.

Anyway, this is kind of giving you an idea of what is happening in this village here.

A glass of my Ford wagon was broken with what seems to be a man's punch. My suspicion was right away set on the drunken man. This is a tented glass of twenty inches by sixty and I am sure it is not a cheap one to replace.

A young man who seems to me very friendly before was passing by the place where I keep my dogs and he stopped to talk to me. We talked about all kind of things when suddenly I asked him to come and look at the broken glass. I put my fist where the glass was hit and I asked him if he too might think this was done with a punch. He also put his punch on the same spot and when he retrieved his hand I noticed he had cuts between each knuckle and all of them very evenly. He then told me he had a fight at a friends' party. I had a lot of fights when I was young, I mean more than anyone I know; so I know for a fact that when you hit someone, you might hurt your knuckles and someone else's mouth, but never between your own knuckles; especially not all of them and evenly, even less like this young man had. One can hit a thousand times in someone's face; he will not get cut between the knuckles, but to punch only one more time in a glass like mine will make the same kind of cuts this young man has on his hand. This man is the son of our new mayor and I still don't know why he would do something like this. I suspected he wanted to steal some of my tools to get him some pocket money and since the doors were locked he would have got mad and hit the glass. His dad is a millionaire, but the boy he's not. He bragged about the hit in the glass being a very good, a very powerful punch.

I told him I had a pretty good idea of who might have done this. Before talking to the cops about this event I thought it was best for me to talk to his father about it and see if we could settle this in a friendly way. This is what I would have liked if my under age son would have done something wrong. I also have a strong suspicion on him about the four magnum wheels and the T-top of my Camero that got stolen behind my house while I was on a trip to BC. Up to ten times a year and this every year since I moved here this young man is saying he is going to buy this car for his young brother. I sincerely think he already has the parts to put back on the car.

Although the new mayor didn't take it well at all and so he let me know. It is one way like any others to encourage the crime. The future will tell.

There is one thing people around here don't seem to know and this is I am under God's protection.

I keep saying to everyone who is willing to hear it that when God pulled me out of British Columbia to bring me to Saskatchewan; He pulled me out of hell to bring me to the kingdom of heaven. I was delivered from a lot of wrong, a lot of bad despite everything is happening over here.

Finally the press conference will only take place once this book is published.

The Judgement and Hell or Heaven

Here are a few visions which were given to me about the judgement and hell. The inhabitants who were lamenting to God still do, but they are lamenting to the devil for now on and really, this is in vain. The devil mocked them all and he is still doing it while laughing, crying and all of this by gnashing his teeth. He is faithful to himself and he listen to no one, but anyway his power is reduced to nothing at all. Before he had to power to tempt the just souls, the righteous, but now he doesn't even have this pleasure anymore. He became very small. He doesn't have any fun anymore with all of his demons who are just as bad as he is. When he looks at others it is just as if he was looking at himself continually. All he sees is ugliness, monstrosity and abyss. All of them see the paradise we have and this in itself is hell for them.

Some of them had the surprise of their life when they got before the judgement. When they appeared before the Great Judge with their little luggage before He who knows and sees everything.

I heard one telling Him she has been faithful all of her life and that she has never quit praying God.

Here is what God had to say to her.

"Yes, I see that you prayed all of your life since you were just a little girl. This gave Me a lot of itches in my ears. I can see that your smile has faded out a little, pretty girl. I heard you pray thousands of times, but not even once for my pleasure. All of your prayers were concentrated on yourself, selfish and proud person that you are. You wanted good notes to look good in class. You wanted nice clothes, so the boys could look at you when you passed by. Then you wanted your parents to stay together, so they can baby you. You prayed for a strong and handsome husband, who doesn't cheat on you and doesn't give you too much trouble. You prayed for good children who don't give you too much sadness. You prayed for good friends, peace and happiness. You prayed for a nice house, a nice car and a big swimming pool." "And You God gave me all those things." "Yes, I gave you all those things that you attached yourself to and when I sent you my servant to ask you to take your little cross and to follow Me (my word), what did you do? You told him; 'Let God talk to me Himself.' And you sent him for a hike. Well, he went and he went to tell other people that I wanted to warn.

Today I'm talking to you as you requested, but you're not going to like what I have to say to you. You have ignored the words that my servant Immanuel suffered to bring you. You also have ignored the law that my servant Moses gave you. You ignored my feasts and my Sabbaths that you celebrated for the pleasure of my enemy, the devil. When you were singing on the day of the sun I was hiding my face away, because I couldn't stand seeing or earring you. You, to whom I gave all those little vagaries of fashion.

I sent you others of my servants to open your eyes. What did you do then? Them too you sent for a hike. Now it is my turn to send you for a hike. Go see in hell, there is a place prepared just for you. It is not the worse, but it is not the best one either. It is the one you deserved though. Although it is far from being like the ones reserved for the people who took their cross and followed, listened and obeyed Me. Go now, go gnash your teeth."

There was also a big fellow I saw in front of the Judge with a big pile of luggage for he was a rich man. He told the Judge all the good things he has done on earth. It was then the Lord told him what his deeds were worth.

"You gave for your own satisfaction to people from whom you expected a return or recognition for your own self-esteem. 'Look at me and see how generous I am.' Do you recognize yourself? Very seldom you gave something you needed for yourself.

You have spread out the lies rather than the truth, that's what your money was used for. You gave thousands and thousands to the beast, but very little to my children. You helped others for your own satisfaction. When finally one of my disciples knocked at your door, what did you do? You threw him out the door and you despised him. You made yourself called child of God, but I'm not your God, I'm not your Father. Your god is the one whom you served. Where is he now? He was happy with you, but I cried over you. Think only of all the money you spent on foolish things. If only this money would have been spent to stop abortion or else to feed the poor in the world; the earth would have been populated a bit more to my liking. You have ignored people in misery even some of your own family.

No, my children didn't do these things. Oh, you were very good at making faces in the assemblies. You were brilliant to disfigure yourself, even though my servant Jesus told you to go in your room to pray." "Yes but, Paul told us to pray everywhere." "What did Immanuel tell you? He told you that if you don't gather with him you were scattering. Why didn't you listen to the one I sent you? You have listened to the one who disguised himself as an angel of heaven to deceive you. You too have listened to the liar, my enemy, the one who worked for your lost.

There is a place prepared for you according to your deeds, but it is not with my children." "Yes but, didn't Jesus die for my sins?" "Jesus sacrificed his life to bring you the truth that you ignored. I'm sorry for you, but you had the opportunity to do the right thing, to spread the truth and you have chosen the liar and his lies. Now go see the one you served, he's happy with you and he is expecting you, but this is not the best place there is."

In conclusion I would like to write you Paul's summary.

Before Paul's supposed conversion to Jesus.

St-Paul, a murderer, a blasphemer, a liar and he forced people to blaspheme. This is proven.

After his supposed conversion to Jesus.

Now all the proofs are in the Bible.

A hypocrite. Proven.

Against circumcision. Proven.

Paul circumcised his disciple, his son Timothy, he who has never touched a woman while he is against circumcision. Proven.

Paul against the Law of God. Proven.

Paul said the Law of God doesn't exist anymore that the Law is the old way, disappeared. He even said the Law of God is a curse. Proven. Is this enough for you?

He contradicted God. Proven.

He contradicted Jesus a lot. Proven.

He fought against Jesus' apostles. Proven.

He put down Jesus' apostles. Proven.

He called himself a father, he who told his disciples it is best not to touch a woman. Proven.

He has also begotten many sons also without touching a woman. Proven.

He condemned. Proven.

He hanged people over to Satan. Proven.

He blasphemed against an angel of heaven. Proven.

He made people blind more than one way. Proven.

He swore. Proven.

He Judged and taught others to judge. Proven.

He called people's names. Proven.

He created the beast number 666. Proven.

He challenged anyone to find the name of the beast. Proven.

He has gossiped. Proven.

He prayed the Lord God three times in an imitation of Jesus to take away from him a messenger of Satan who kept him from becoming conceited. Satan who is the most conceited being. This is quite something in the Bible. Proven.

According to the scripture Paul never did repent either. Why Satan, the devil who is the king of false pride repent of anything? He is way too conceited to do this. Proven.

Now, would you tell me, you all the Christians in the world that Paul is your director? Isn't it the Holy Bible the book of the truth?

The proofs are there in the Bible and I write them in my books. Is this a crime deserving death? I would say it is as it was for Louis Riel, at least for the Christians churches.

From James Prince, a Jesus' disciple!